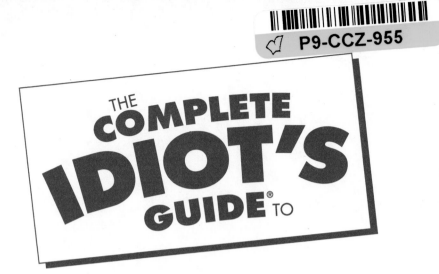

P9-CCZ-955

THE COMPLETE IDIOT'S GUIDE® TO

Baby Sign Language

Second Edition

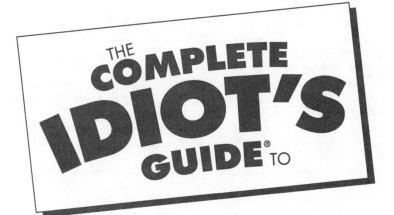

THE COMPLETE IDIOT'S GUIDE® TO

Baby Sign Language

Second Edition

by Diane Ryan

ALPHA

A member of Penguin Group (USA) Inc.

ALPHA BOOKS

Published by the Penguin Group

Penguin Group (USA) Inc., 375 Hudson Street, New York, New York 10014, USA

Penguin Group (Canada), 90 Eglinton Avenue East, Suite 700, Toronto, Ontario M4P 2Y3, Canada (a division of Pearson Penguin Canada Inc.)

Penguin Books Ltd., 80 Strand, London WC2R 0RL, England

Penguin Ireland, 25 St. Stephen's Green, Dublin 2, Ireland (a division of Penguin Books Ltd.)

Penguin Group (Australia), 250 Camberwell Road, Camberwell, Victoria 3124, Australia (a division of Pearson Australia Group Pty. Ltd.)

Penguin Books India Pvt. Ltd., 11 Community Centre, Panchsheel Park, New Delhi—110 017, India

Penguin Group (NZ), 67 Apollo Drive, Rosedale, North Shore, Auckland 1311, New Zealand (a division of Pearson New Zealand Ltd.)

Penguin Books (South Africa) (Pty.) Ltd., 24 Sturdee Avenue, Rosebank, Johannesburg 2196, South Africa

Penguin Books Ltd., Registered Offices: 80 Strand, London WC2R 0RL, England

International Standard Book Number: 978-1-59257-862-7
Library of Congress Catalog Card Number: 2008933154

11 10 09   8 7 6 5 4 3 2

Interpretation of the printing code: The rightmost number of the first series of numbers is the year of the book's printing; the rightmost number of the second series of numbers is the number of the book's printing. For example, a printing code of 09-1 shows that the first printing occurred in 2009.

Printed in the United States of America

Note: This publication contains the opinions and ideas of its author. It is intended to provide helpful and informative material on the subject matter covered. It is sold with the understanding that the author and publisher are not engaged in rendering professional services in the book. If the reader requires personal assistance or advice, a competent professional should be consulted.

The author and publisher specifically disclaim any responsibility for any liability, loss, or risk, personal or otherwise, which is incurred as a consequence, directly or indirectly, of the use and application of any of the contents of this book.

Most Alpha books are available at special quantity discounts for bulk purchases for sales promotions, premiums, fund-raising, or educational use. Special books, or book excerpts, can also be created to fit specific needs.

For details, write: Special Markets, Alpha Books, 375 Hudson Street, New York, NY 10014.

Publisher: *Marie Butler-Knight*
Editorial Director: *Mike Sanders*
Senior Managing Editor: *Billy Fields*
Acquisitions Editor: *Michele Wells*
Development Editor: *Lynn Northrup*
Production Editor: *Megan Douglass*

Copy Editor: *Jan Zoya*
Cover Designer: *Becky Harmon*
Book Designer: *Trina Wurst*
Layout: *Chad Dressler*
Proofreader: *Mary Hunt, Megan Wade*

Contents at a Glance

Contents

Appendixes

Introduction

Once upon a not-so-long-ago time, a book that taught you how to communicate with babies before they could speak would have been found in the Occult or Science Fiction section of the bookstore. But now that the subject has gone mainstream, here it sits next to all the other books on ways to be a better parent.

Actually, the word *mainstream* doesn't quite cut it. It's far too tame. Signing with hearing babies has become a national—even international—phenomenon! It's on the news, in magazines, and even in the movies. "It's something you can't afford *not* to do," your friends tell you. "But then your baby won't talk!" says your mother-in-law. Who's a parent to believe?

The questions are swirling around in your head. Is signing with a hearing baby really a good idea? Yes, say the experts. But not that long ago, some Chinese guru thought that binding a baby's feet was inspired. And what about the practical issues? Do you have time to do this? Will you have to learn a complete sign language when you had trouble with pig Latin in grade school? And what happens if you start signing and then decide to stop? Will your baby stutter? Or what if he gets *too good* at it and your mother-in-law is right? Maybe he won't speak at all!

Lots to think about, huh? If you're like most parents, you've already been online looking for more information. What did you find? Too many opinions and too many products, plus scads of stuff about creating smarter babies. Is baby sign language part of that, too?

That's another thing. When did we all get so competitive? Can't we just relax and enjoy our babies? Do we have to send in his application to Harvard before he's out of diapers? What if he'd prefer Yale? This is just too much for a parent to take! Can't anyone help?

That's where I come in.

Okay, so who am I and what can I offer? Allow me to answer the second question first: illumination, perspective, education, and guidance.

Now for the introduction: my name is Diane Ryan and I'm someone who has asked the very same questions that you're asking right now. But because I'm also a speech and language pathologist, my skepticism and concerns motivated me to dig deeper. So I studied the research, read the reports, reviewed the programs, talked to parents, tested what worked and what didn't, and created a program of my own.

Since I founded KinderSigns eight years ago, I've personally taught hundreds of parents to teach their hearing babies to sign, both here in the United States and in Europe. Thousands more have learned through my online programs. Plus, I've created an international network of instructors who now teach the KinderSigns technique in their own communities worldwide. So when it comes to finding an expert on the subject of teaching your hearing baby to sign, you don't have to look any further.

This second edition of *The Complete Idiot's Guide to Baby Sign Language* is an encore performance for me with Alpha Books. When Alpha contacted me to write the first edition in 2006, I asked myself, "Does the world need another book on how to teach sign language to babies?" Apparently it did and still does. Since that time, a lot has happened. More books on the subject have been published; more DVDs have come out—and there's been important research that you need to know about, all of which is included in this new edition. There are new signs to teach and a new potty training program to make your life easier. There's even a special appendix to help Dad play a more active role in teaching his baby to sign.

Once again, as in the first edition, my goal is to dispel the myths, validate the truths, discuss the programs, convince you to sign with your baby, and then teach you how. You know those friends of yours who told you that signing with your hearing baby is something you can't afford *not* to do? Well, they were absolutely right.

There is one particular addition to this book of which I am most proud. It's called "The Baby Sign Language Express." Simply put, it's a way for you to teach your baby to sign in two weeks or less. While this is not a new discovery, it is the first time, to my knowledge, that anyone has presented the material in such a way. For those who thought they didn't have the time or the patience to sign with their babies, Chapter 5 is for you.

Please note: throughout this book (for the sake of simplicity and my sanity), I have used the pronouns *he* or *him* when referring to babies rather than the awkward *he/she* combination. This deference to the masculine gender in no way reflects any bias or negativity toward baby girls. In fact, I had two of my own. Hi, Michelle and Kristin!

How to Use This Book

The book is divided into three parts:

Part 1, "Baby Sign Language Basics," separates facts from fiction and offers a solid foundation for your learning experience. You'll meet the researchers, study the benefits, and learn why teaching your baby to sign is a priceless gift to give your child.

Part 2, "Ready, Set, Sign!" provides everything you need to know to get started. You'll learn what signs to teach your baby and exactly how to teach him. Plus you'll discover that teaching your baby to sign is much easier than you thought. In this section you will also find the "Baby Sign Language Express" program, the fastest way to teach your hearing baby to sign.

Part 3, "The Advanced Signer," is for those who want to continue signing into the toddler stage and beyond. You'll discover tips and techniques unique to this age group, including how to use sign language when potty training. And if you're wondering what to do when your little one starts talking, in Part 3 you'll find out how speech and sign language complement one another.

In addition, you'll find the following:

- **Baby Sign Language Dictionary.** Here you'll find more than 120 of the most popular signs to teach your baby. Each illustration clearly demonstrates how to make the sign and comes complete with written instructions to make the job even easier. The dictionary is divided into categories to help you decide which signs you want to teach your baby or toddler. I'm certain that you'll come to appreciate this valuable resource at every stage of your signing adventure.

- **Appendix A, "Dad's Corner."** Don't feel left out, Dad! There are many things you can do to speed up the process and bond with your baby at the same time. This special appendix is just for you.

- **Appendix B, "Questions I'm Asked the Most."** Have a question? There's a good chance that someone has already asked it. I'll answer the most popular questions here.

- ◆ **Appendix C, "Fun and Games."** Signing with your baby has to be fun. This appendix offers suggestions on how to reinforce the signs you teach and have a great time while you're at it. Plus you'll find valuable suggestions on other ways to stimulate your baby's brain.

- ◆ **Appendix D, "Resources."** While this book is all you need to teach your baby to sign, you'll find other helpful resources in this appendix, including baby sign language forums, informational websites, and other publications to enhance your learning and teaching experience.

- ◆ **Appendix E, "Baby Sign Language Journal."** Keep track of your baby's signing progress by entering the date that you introduce a sign and the date your baby learns it. Clip out the journal and keep it handy to update babysitters and caregivers on your baby's progress.

Extras

Throughout this book, you'll also find sidebars that offer tips, cautions, and other tidbits of information:

Smart Signs

Check these boxes for tips and tidbits to make things go more smoothly and guarantee signing success.

Take Note

Here you'll find words of caution about how to avoid roadblocks and stay on track.

Behind the Signs

Check these boxes for interesting facts on the subject of babies and sign language. Great material for your next cocktail party!

Acknowledgments

Completing a project like this wasn't as easy as I thought it would be. In fact, it wouldn't have happened at all if it were not for the efforts of a special few: the editors of Alpha Books, especially Lynn Northrup, who honed my copy and made it better. Carolyn Barcomb, artist extraordinaire, who added warmth and personality to the illustrations. Steve Remington, my consultant and sage business manager. Michelle Rowley and Kristin Hanratty, my smart and successful daughters, for their encouragement and support. And most especially, to my husband Bob. No words can express my gratitude for who you are, and what you have done and continue to do for me each and every day of my life.

Special Thanks to the Technical Reviewer

The Complete Idiot's Guide to Baby Sign Language, Second Edition, was reviewed by an expert who double-checked the accuracy of what you'll learn here, to help us ensure that this book gives you everything you need to know about signing with your baby. Special thanks are extended to Cheryl Bavaro.

Cheryl Bavaro has degrees in Early Elementary Education and Child Psychology from Penn State, as well as certifications in Child Day Care and Day Care Management. The owner of Cheryl's Kid Konnection, an in-home day care center, she is also mom to Nathan and Colby. She has been teaching baby sign language for three years, and in her spare time she enjoys spending time with her children and husband John.

Trademarks

All terms mentioned in this book that are known to be or are suspected of being trademarks or service marks have been appropriately capitalized, including KinderSigns™, *Sign with Your Baby*™, and *Baby Signs*®. Alpha Books and Penguin Group (USA) Inc. cannot attest to the accuracy of this information. Use of a term in this book should not be regarded as affecting the validity of any trademark or service mark.

Part 1

Baby Sign Language Basics

Just when you thought that raising your hand to a child was a possible felony, along comes a school of thought that not only tells you that you *should*—but that your child will be much better off if you do. Tough love? No. Baby sign language.

You've heard about it, read about it, seen it on TV or maybe in the movies. It is, after all, an intriguing idea. Imagine, communicating with a baby before that baby can actually speak!

"Ridiculous!" your great-grandmother would have said. "Not a good idea," according to your mother-in-law. "Worth the effort?" you're asking yourself.

In Part 1, I'll answer the questions and address the concerns. The big one, of course, is why would anyone want to teach sign language to a *hearing* child? Can it, in fact, impede a baby's normal development?

Some of the answers will surprise you; others may intrigue you. Together, I hope they will motivate you to learn more about an innovative way to communicate with your baby— through sign language.

1

What's All the Fuss About?

In This Chapter

- ◆ Discovering what baby sign language is—and what it isn't
- ◆ Learning what it will and won't do
- ◆ Understanding how hearing babies benefit from learning sign language
- ◆ Meeting the people behind the signs and the science
- ◆ Making the decision: to sign or not to sign?

Congratulations! You are an open-minded parent, a person who hears about something unusual and wants to know more. Maybe you heard about signing with babies at your cousin Shelly's baby shower. But as you soon discovered, showers aren't ideal settings for in-depth discussions. Everyone's real focus is on those fabulous games and oohing and ahhing over the baby gifts.

Or maybe TV news was your source. There was a whopping 60 seconds devoted to the concept one night. Remember, it was right after the Washington scandal and before the Wall Street report? Interesting information, to be sure. But are you going to make a decision as important as this based on an info-minute?

So hats off to you! You've done the responsible thing and are investigating the idea firsthand. You'll make an excellent parent, if you haven't already achieved that status.

I assume you're ready, then? Highlighter uncapped? You're about to learn all there is to know about teaching a hearing baby to sign.

Exactly What Is Baby Sign Language?

Simply put, baby sign language is a way to communicate with your baby before your baby can speak by teaching him a few basic gestures or signs. It's a way to bridge the gap between his gurgling stages to the time when he can actually talk. Some parents continue well beyond that stage. That's optional.

In fact, there are a number of options available to you when it comes to signing. One has to do with why you want to do it in the first place. If you're like most parents, you're considering it as an interim method of communication before your baby's first words. Other parents think of it as a way to begin a lifelong skill. There's one thing everyone needs to agree upon, however. In order to be successful, it has to be fun for all involved.

Now let's talk about what baby sign language *isn't*. It is not part of "Super Baby" mania, the craze to create smarter, higher-thinking infants and children. And while you may find baby sign language books, tapes, and DVDs in the same aisle as the so-called IQ-boosters, they're not in the same ballpark. Research now tells us that all the music and mental stimulation programs don't do much more than entertain a baby. In order to boost mental acuity, human interaction needs to be part of the learning environment. And human interaction is what signing with your baby is all about.

Now, in the interest of full disclosure, I should tell you that there are some differences of opinion as to how much of an IQ boost sign language really creates. Some say not much at all; others say as much as a 20-point gain. But, as I often tell parents, even if you totally discount a higher IQ as a signing advantage, there are still numerous other reasons why it's still an incredible idea.

Parents feel good about teaching a baby to sign because it's natural. It's based on an instinctive tendency to gesture. It also enhances communication, builds stronger connections in families, and reduces a preverbal baby's frustration when he can't get his point across. Those are the primary reasons why you should sign with your baby. It will help you develop a closer relationship with your little one and form a tighter bond. Plus, your baby will really love the experience! If there are cerebral fringe benefits beyond that—and most scientists tell us that there are—then all the better.

A Simple and Natural Way to Communicate

Teaching a baby to sign is simple. It's about as far from rocket science as you can get. Yes, it does involve some patience and dedication, but there's a huge payoff at the end of the day and it's well worth your investment. At the very least, it's something you should seriously consider.

When you teach your baby to sign, you will use signs that are part of American Sign Language (ASL), the official language of the deaf community in the United States. While some signs have been adapted to make them easier for a baby to make, the majority are the "genuine articles." That explains why many parents consider this as the first step in introducing a second language to their child.

Oh, I'm *so* sorry! To the lady who's hyperventilating in Houston, let me clarify that last statement. Yes, you will be using authentic ASL signs, but you *don't* have to learn an entire sign language! You'll start with a few basic signs and can add as many as you like from there. Feel better?

Behind the Signs

According to Hollywood magazines, even the stars are signing with their babies. Debra Messing, Julia Roberts, and Nicole Ritchie are baby sign language supporters. Plus Robert DeNiro taught a few signs to his on-screen grandson in the 2005 film *Meet the Fockers*.

Here's something else you might not have thought about. Depending on your baby's age, he may already *be* signing! Babies raise their hands to be picked up. They point to things they want. And think how easy it is to teach a baby to wave "bye-bye." That means when you teach your baby to sign, you are simply taking advantage of what comes naturally.

Is it essential that you teach your baby to sign? No. Will your baby suffer if you don't? Well, maybe *suffer* isn't the right word, but he (and you) will miss out on a closer connection, plus a host of other astonishing benefits if you pass it up.

Think of this as a golden opportunity. Actually, it's much more valuable than gold. It's a priceless opportunity to find out what your baby is thinking. It's a way to look into his world through *his* eyes. Why just guess at what your baby wants or needs? If you teach him to sign, he can tell you himself.

When you teach your baby to sign you don't have to wait until he's ready to communicate with words. That could be months away. Think of all the time you may be wasting! (Especially when you factor in the teenage years when he probably won't speak to you at all.) So give your baby the tools he needs to communicate and start a two-way dialogue—*right now.*

Why Teach Sign Language to a Hearing Baby?

It used to be that sign language was associated only with the deaf culture. No one saw the benefits of teaching sign language to hearing children. After all, what was the purpose? They would speak eventually. And then someone came along who thought outside the box. That's how good ideas usually happen. In this case, it was an extraordinary one.

While working as an interpreter for the deaf in Alaska in the late 1970s, Joseph Garcia noticed that the hearing babies of deaf parents communicated at a much earlier age than children of hearing parents. That observation piqued his interest, sparked additional research, and resulted in a practical system to teach the technique to parents. We'll learn more about Garcia and his "Sign with Your Baby" program later in this chapter. But for now we should credit Garcia with rephrasing the question that we started with. Instead of asking *why* anyone would want to teach sign language to hearing babies, Garcia asked, "Why not?"

Some might say, "I'll tell you why not. Don't I have enough to do? Plus, I already know what my baby wants and needs. I can tell by the way he cries. His hunger cry is different from his cry for attention. And when he's in pain, I can tell that, too."

There is a lot of truth to that, of course. Mothers, especially, have a sixth sense when it comes to interpreting their baby's cries and body language. But a *signing* baby can share more *specific* information about what he wants or needs, plus he'll scoop up a host of secondary benefits along the way.

Speaking of benefits, we'll delve into them (and the supporting research) more specifically later on, but for now, let me tantalize you with this. Babies who sign ...

- Are less frustrated.
- Have closer bonds with their parents and caregivers.
- Develop larger vocabularies.
- Become better readers.
- "Outsmart" babies who don't sign.

 Take Note

While baby sign language has long-term intellectual and emotional advantages for your baby, your primary reason for signing should be to have a less frustrated, well-adjusted child. Plus, it's fun!

The Biggest Misconception

Is there a downside to teaching your baby sign language? I know what you're thinking. It's the number-one question I get. And the answer is a resounding *no!* What you *really* want to know is, "If I teach my baby to sign, won't his speech be delayed?"

In fact, just the opposite is true. If you teach your baby a few simple signs, he'll speak *earlier.* And that's *sign-tifically* proven! (More on that later.) Now you can add *earlier speech* to the list of benefits I just mentioned.

Your question, by the way, is a good one. It's logical to think that by teaching your baby to sign you might be giving him a reason not to talk. But let's look down the road a bit further.

When you introduce a specific sign to your baby, you will *talk* to him at the same time. Rule #1 is that you must always *say* the word as you make the sign. You never sign without speaking.

And there's this: research tells us that parents of signing babies spend more time with them. Suddenly "babydom" takes on a new dimension. It becomes less custodial. Signing babies can actually *participate* in the family dynamic. The family spends more time with him playing, reading, labeling things, asking him questions, responding to those same questions, and talking and talking ... Beginning to get the picture?

Smart Signs

Don't listen to those who tell you that sign language will delay your baby's language development. Just the opposite is true. Signing babies speak earlier than those who don't. And that's a fact!

What Will Your Baby Be Able to Tell You?

Maybe this will help convey the idea. Let's visit the Humdrum household. They've never heard about baby sign language.

It's 2:30 A.M. and 12-month-old Amanda starts to cry. Mom gets up and goes to her room. She goes through the mental checklist. She feels Amanda's diaper. Totally dry. She offers her some water. Amanda cries even louder. She puts her lips to the baby's forehead. No fever. Now Amanda is screaming. And Mrs. H. is starting to panic.

Meet the Seinworthys. They live right down the street from the Humdrums and, you guessed it, they know all about baby sign language. In fact, they have been signing with little Bradley since he was seven months old. Let's take the same scenario and see how it applies to them.

It's 2:30 A.M. and 12-month-old Bradley starts to cry. Mom gets up and goes to his room. She goes through the mental checklist. She feels Bradley's diaper. Totally dry. She offers him some water. Bradley cries even louder. She puts her lips to the baby's forehead. No fever. Now Bradley is screaming.

Mrs. Seinworthy puts her two index fingers together in Bradley's sightline. It's the sign for "pain." Bradley makes the same sign in front of his mouth. Mom realizes that he's teething again. She gets his medicine and rubs it on his gums. A few minutes later, Bradley stops crying and falls back asleep. And Mrs. S. goes back to bed.

Pretty amazing, don't you think? A baby who can sign can tell you when he's in pain and also *where it hurts!* He can tell you when he's hungry, thirsty, and if he needs help. And get this, he can even tell you when he needs a diaper change! Truly extraordinary—especially when you consider that a baby can "tell" you all these things before he is able to utter a single word.

How Is All This Possible?

Research has shown that while babies lack the fine motor skills to speak, they do have the ability to understand and use language as early as six to seven months—if they are given the right tools and guidance. While speech may be more than six months away, a baby's receptive language skills significantly improve after only six months on the planet. So has his ability to manipulate objects with his hands. Why wait for your baby to speak his first words? He may be ready to communicate *now!*

Speaking of *speaking*, think about how really complicated the act of talking is, especially to a baby. To us, it's second nature. We have something to say and out it comes. But speech is an intricate and exacting dance.

Depending on the sounds or words you want to say, your tongue must be in a precise location, your lips need to coordinate with your teeth, and you have to control your breathing to direct the flow of air, all the while making sure that you have enough left over so you don't pass out. Whew! A baby's brain needs about a year or more to even begin to take on that task!

But wait! That's just on the mechanical side. Before your baby says his first word, he needs to hear that word many times and have some idea of its meaning. He has to be able to differentiate between sounds and words, plus recognize where words begin and end. We Americans don't pause very long in between words, you know. To a baby, a family discussion sounds like a constant stream of gibberish. But somehow—miraculously—and in such a very short period of time, a baby will sort it all out and be able to speak. How can you help him simplify and accelerate the process? By helping him learn a few basic signs.

Can All Babies Do This?

As you know, gesturing is a natural tendency for a baby. It's something that he'll do even if you don't follow through with this program. Babies are mimics. They take their lead from the people who surround them. They learn to speak by listening to you. And they'll learn to sign by watching you.

So whether or not a baby will sign has little to do with the baby. All babies can learn to sign. How fast they'll learn and how many signs they'll make are the things in question. But you already know the variable, right? The degree of signing success a baby achieves is in direct proportion to the level of dedication and enthusiasm of his parents!

By the way, I've taught baby sign language for eight years in the United States and Europe and have never heard any parents say that their baby just couldn't grasp the concept. While there are obvious differences in every baby's ability, all babies can learn to sign.

Is This Appropriate for Deaf Babies, Too?

As I've mentioned, some parents have long-range intentions when they start teaching their baby sign language. But most parents will only sign until their baby's speech surpasses his signing ability. A deaf baby, obviously, has a much greater challenge than a hearing child. He needs a lifelong skill to be able to communicate. Whether a deaf baby is taught lip reading or sign language or a combination of both, he needs a more structured program specifically designed for that tiny individual and his particular level of hearing loss.

The techniques that are presented in this book are designed to enhance a baby's ability to communicate, not establish it. These demonstrations are based on the premise that the baby has the ability to hear and will eventually produce the sounds and words that are being presented to him. Will teaching these signs to a deaf baby hurt him? Of course not. But this program doesn't go far enough, nor is it comprehensive enough to address a deaf baby's special needs.

Back to the Beginning

Maybe you're the type of person who doesn't care about the origin of things. To you, Darwin's no big deal. You live in the present and don't like to look back. If that sounds like you, skip this part. It isn't mandatory reading.

But if you're like I was at first, you may still be somewhat skeptical. You need more information—especially when your baby is involved.

Who are these people who cooked up this idea? What are their credentials? Do these so-called experts really have something important to say, or are they just trying to stretch their 15 minutes of fame to an hour?

So let's back up to the beginning and meet the baby sign language pioneers. At the very least, it's interesting reading. You may even be able to use some of it when there's a lull at your next cocktail party. And who knows? One day you might be a contestant on *Jeopardy* when the category pops up. ("I'll take Baby Sign Language Pioneers for $500, Alex.")

The Prime Mover

The interest in teaching sign language to hearing babies began in the late 1980s with two separate and significant research projects conducted by Joseph Garcia, a student at Alaska Pacific University, whom you met a few pages ago, and the team of Linda Acredolo and Susan Goodwyn, then Ph.D.s at University of California, Davis. While their research was independent and distinct, the three had one thing in common. They used what they had around the house to formulate and test their theories: their kids.

Behind the Signs

American Sign Language (ASL) is used in the United States and in English-speaking Canada. Many countries have their own sign language and some, like British Sign Language (BSL), have dialects. That means someone in London signs differently than a guy wearing a kilt in Scotland.

As an undergraduate student, Joseph Garcia became fascinated with the idea of communicating through gestures or signs. While no one was deaf in his family, he thought that learning sign language would be interesting and he began to study it in earnest. Once he had a solid grasp of American Sign Language (ASL), Garcia was certified as an interpreter for the deaf and became involved, both personally and professionally, with the deaf community. It resulted in an observation that changed his life—and the lives of many to come.

While spending time with deaf friends, Garcia noticed that the normal-hearing babies of deaf parents were able to communicate basic wants and needs at around 10 months of age. How was that possible? Simple. Their parents had taught them a few basic signs.

Garcia contrasted this with the communicative ability of hearing babies with hearing parents. Around that age (10 months), they hardly communicated at all! Intrigued by this disparity, Garcia decided to make it the focus of his Master's thesis.

During his research, Garcia discovered that hearing children were able to produce simple signs at around eight months and some exceptional children as early as six months. Certainly this was far earlier than any baby could articulate any *spoken* word.

Garcia also found that once a signing child began to speak, he had a better grasp of grammar and language in general. Using his infant sons Stratton and Damien as "test subjects," Garcia validated his theories firsthand on the home front.

Joseph Garcia's program evolved into the popular book/video program, *Sign with Your Baby: How to Communicate with Infants Before They Can Speak* (see Appendix D). Like this program, it's based on using American Sign Language as the basis for communicating with a baby through signing. For more information, visit www.sign2me.com.

Behind the Signs

There is evidence that sign language benefited the hearing community before the sixteenth century. During that time, Benedictine monks used sign language to communicate with one another when they observed long periods of silence.

The Doctors in the House

The findings of the Acredolo-Goodwyn team also stemmed from simple observations. In 1982 when her daughter Kate was a year old, psychology professor Linda Acredolo noticed that she was making an "itsy bitsy spider" with her hands whenever she saw one of the critters. When Kate spotted a flower, she would wiggle her nose as if sniffing it. Then there was a third event, one that's especially interesting.

It was time for Kate's 12-month checkup at the pediatrician's office. While they were in the waiting room, Kate was naturally attracted by the large aquarium there and toddled over for a better look. But then, according to Linda, she did something strange. She started to *blow*.

Dr. Mom was puzzled by the behavior. After the appointment she took Kate home for a nap. As she put her down in her crib, Linda "activated" the mobile that hung over it. It was fashioned of brightly colored fish—and in order to make it rotate, Linda had to blow on it. Instantly, she became aware of the connection her daughter had made. Without any instruction, Kate was communicating with her own form of sign language.

As you might imagine, the learned professor wanted to find out more. She had lots of questions:

- Do all children do this or just my daughter?

- Are there other signs or gestures Kate might be using that I'm unaware of?

- Can I become an expert on this, create a national phenomenon, appear on *Oprah*, and make a fortune?

 Smart Signs

Notice how simple observation is key to learning and discovery? Like Linda Acredolo, pay close attention to your own baby. See if he is making signs or gestures on his own. If he is, that's a sure sign that he's ready to learn others.

(Okay, I made up that last one—but that's just what happened.)

And so her quest began. Linda partnered with her colleague, Susan Goodwyn, then professor of psychology and child development at California University, Stanislaus, and an associate researcher at the University of California. Together they studied, observed, and questioned other parents. As scientists, they did things the right way. Backed by a federal grant, they compared babies who signed with babies who didn't. Then they followed and documented their progress. We'll look into those findings in greater detail in the next chapter.

Based on Acredolo and Goodwyn's research, *Baby Signs: How to Talk with Your Baby Before Your Baby Can Talk* (see Appendix D) was published. The program promotes a short-term sign language experience and recommends a combination of baby-friendly ASL plus signs and gestures that parents and babies develop use on their own. For more information visit www.babysigns.com.

There are many baby sign language books and tapes available that are based on the findings of the baby sign language pioneers. No matter which program you use, remember that your final goal is not just to get your baby to sign, but to *speak*.

What's the Deal with Dunstan?

In the beginning of this chapter, I mentioned that parents have an instinctive ability to interpret what their babies are crying about. Moms especially seem have this innate ability. But I thought I would mention another mother who says she has more sophisticated interpretive powers than most. You may have heard of Priscilla Dunstan or have seen her on *Oprah*.

Dunstan is an Australian opera singer who claims to have a photographic memory for sound. When she was five, as the story goes, she was able to play back Mozart symphonies note for note on her violin after having heard them only once.

Dunstan states that she used her unique memory skills to closely monitor and remember her baby's cries and how he responded to various interventions—like feeding, burping, or changing his diaper. (I think they're called "nappies" in Australia.) Then she studied other babies and found that they all responded in similar ways to similar wants and needs. In her DVD program, *The Dunstan Baby System*, she teaches parents how they can interpret their own baby's cries.

Does the program work? Frankly, I don't know. Critics initially stated that there wasn't enough research, and in my opinion, the claim that all babies have common speech/language cues is somewhat extreme. Also a bit unnerving are the sounds, actually *noises*, that you need to practice yourself to help you understand your baby.

Smart Signs

The old school of thought was that you should let a baby cry for a while so as not to spoil him. My advice? Better to take a chance on a spoiled child than one who thinks his cries have no effect on you at all.

I mention the Dunstan system here because I have been asked a lot about it and whether or not it fits in with teaching your baby sign language. My response is that it's like comparing an apple and an orange. Regardless, it should in no way replace baby sign language and could divert your energies away from it. With Dunstan's program you are the interpreter. When your baby signs, he plays the dominant role because he is the one communicating his needs, wants, and ideas. That, I feel, is of much, much greater value. If you want to check it out for yourself, visit www.dunstanbaby.com.

Why Listen to Me?

While the baby sign language programs I've just discussed are excellent resources, you've purchased this book instead. Let me assure you that it's all you'll need. My experience as a speech and language pathologist, combined with simple teaching style, add up to the proven, easy-to-understand KinderSigns method. Since 2001, parents and childcare professionals in over 40 countries worldwide have used my approach to teach babies sign language. Some parents have even "gone professional" and started their own business as KinderSigns instructors. (For more information, visit www.kindersigns.com.)

The other reason you should listen to me is because I care. I really do. When you come down to it, I suppose you could say that I am a self-proclaimed evangelist when it comes to signing with babies. (I bet you never would have guessed.) The results never cease to amaze me. Here's an example ...

Last week I was at the airport picking up my daughter who was making her annual winter journey from Michigan to Florida. (Our guest room is booked solid in the winter; summertime no one wants to know us.) I got on the elevator from the parking garage, and a mom and dad got on with their 13-month-old in a stroller. (I asked.) As we went from level to level, the little guy's sandal fell off. Because his parents were looking the other way, I picked it up and held it in front of him and said, "Look what you lost!" The little one looked at me and made the sign for "shoe." It just took me by surprise. Of course I did what I tell everyone they should do when their baby makes a sign: I got all excited, repeated the word and the sign, and put his shoe back on—after I got the parents' permission, of course.

The story gets better—and somewhat embarrassing. We all got off at the same terminal level and I asked how they knew about signing. They told me they had read a great book and, yes, I swear, it was mine. Now they got all excited asked me for my autograph and took my picture with the baby. But there's more. A local news crew happened to be in the airport covering the usual stuff, probably about air traffic delays, and one of the parents said to the reporter, "Hey, we have a celebrity here!"

The reporter and cameraperson stopped and asked who I was. Well, trying to explain baby signing in a 10-second sound bite is like trying to stuff one of the ugly stepsister's feet in Cinderella's shoe. But I did my best.

Now the dream ending here would be that I appeared on the evening news, received numerous phone calls, which resulted in major publicity and my book sales skyrocketed. The truth is I never made it on the news. But that was okay. I've been on TV before and I was having a bad hair day so it was just as well. (You can see how I'm compensating.) But the thrill of the day for me was seeing that baby sign. And I had played a major role in teaching that baby how to do it. It really felt good.

The Least You Need to Know

- Baby sign language is a way to communicate with a hearing baby before the baby can speak.

- While there are many benefits, the primary reason to sign with a baby is to reduce the baby's frustration and to promote a closer parental bond.

- Joseph Garcia is largely credited with first discovering that babies can communicate through sign language before they can speak.

- The spontaneous signs her daughter made prompted Linda Acredolo, Ph.D., to partner with fellow Ph.D. Susan Goodwyn to conduct research into the baby sign language phenomenon.

- The method you will learn in this book is based on the KinderSigns program and utilizes ASL.

- This book's sign language range and teaching methodology is not comprehensive enough to be used as an educational tool for the deaf or hard of hearing.

Chapter 2

How Your Baby (and You) Will Benefit

In This Chapter

- ◆ Learning more about the researchers
- ◆ Marveling at their discoveries
- ◆ Learning the benefits of baby sign language
- ◆ Ridding yourself of all doubt

Welcome to "Baby Sign Language University," the most cerebral part of the book. You met some of the "faculty" during orientation in the previous chapter. In case you were absent that day and no one took notes for you, we talked about how the idea of preverbal communication with babies got started. Like you, everyone was skeptical at first. All good scientists are. But they poked, postulated, and finally pronounced that teaching sign language to a hearing baby was a sound proposition—with benefits too amazing to pass up.

Now it's time to take a closer look at how our learned scholars arrived at their conclusions. Then we'll talk about how you and your baby will benefit from what they found. This is important information, class, so pay attention!

A Cinematic Approach

In our last chapter, you were introduced to Linda Acredolo and Susan Goodwyn, both Ph.D.s with a host of other impressive credentials. We talked about how Linda's daughter's spontaneous attempts at signing prompted two decades of research with her learned colleague. While there have been other studies in the field, their research has been the most publicized.

Because any research can be dry and hard to swallow, let me try to make it more palatable for you. If Hollywood were to take this material and make it into a major blockbuster, they would first need financial backing. So did Acredolo and Goodwyn. In 1989, they headed for the National Institute of Health and managed to convince potential backers that studying the long-term effects of teaching hearing babies sign language was worthy of a grant. Their earlier research had convinced the dynamic duo of the short-term benefits. Now they needed to know more.

The Premise:

It was a simple one, really, presented in the form of a question. What were the advantages (or disadvantages) of teaching sign language to hearing babies?

The Players:

Over 140 families with 11-month-old babies were cast. Each family had to fit a certain criteria to make sure that they were all at a similar stage of development. Family income and education were considered as well as each baby's sex, birth order, and ability to vocalize.

The Plot:

One-third of the families were shown how to use sign language. Another third were encouraged to speak to their babies more often than they would normally. The remaining families were the control group. They were told to simply do what comes naturally, to continue caring for their babies as they would normally. None of the groups was aware of the other participants and no one had any idea what the whole thing was about.

The Contract:

Each family agreed to spend two years under the microscope. If this were TV, it would be like a reality show without the cameras. Their progress would be monitored, and after 24 months the signing babies would be tested to see if there were any benefits or negative side-effects. Then comparisons would be made with the other groups.

> **Take Note**
>
> Keep in mind that the results mentioned in these studies are based on the "average" and will not be the same for each child. That means that your baby may not reach these lofty heights. He could soar even higher!

The Exciting Conclusion:

◆ At 24 months, the signing babies had the vocabularies of 27- or 28-month-olds.

◆ At 24 months, they used significantly longer sentences.

◆ At 36 months, the signers spoke like 47-month-olds. Almost a full year ahead!

Bottom line? The signing babies outperformed and outclassed all other groups in the study.

The Sequel:

Pretty impressive, don't you think? But the learned ladies didn't stop there. Scientists always want to know more. In this case it was whether or not there would be any *long-term* effects to teaching a hearing baby to sign. So what did they do? They waited eight years and paid those same families another visit.

The children, now age eight, were tested to see what happened after all that time. Were there any long-term benefits? Were there any "bad seeds" in the bunch?

> **Smart Signs**
>
> Your IQ is determined by multiplying your mental age by 100 and then dividing it by your chronological age. For example, if your two-year-old has the intellectual level of a three-year-old, his IQ is 150. One smart kid! (By the way, IQ is an indication of your *ability to learn*, not how smart you are.)

The Reviews:

Two thumbs up. Way up! The reviews were all positive. In general, when tested eight years later, babies who had learned some basic sign language had better language and cognitive skills than those who hadn't.

◆ Signing babies had an average IQ of 114 compared with 102 for their nonsigning counterparts.

◆ Signing babies demonstrated an above-average understanding of English, plus their grammar and syntax were more advanced.

Added Star Power

While Acredolo and Goodwyn are the best-known "celebrities" in the field, having promoted their findings on the talk-show circuit, there's another star on the Walk of Fame who can't be ignored.

Marilyn Daniels (Maltese), Ph.D., then professor of Communication Arts and Sciences at Penn State University, is probably the most prolific researcher on the subject of children and sign language that we have today. While she acknowledged the Acredolo-Goodwyn studies, she decided to dig deeper into the correlation between sign language and intellectual and academic development.

Dr. Daniels's research stemmed from an observation her graduate students made. They wondered why the hearing children of deaf parents seemed to do so well in reading and writing. Logical thinking told them that because these children lived in a language-deprived environment, they should be struggling in these areas, not excelling in them.

And so Dr. Daniels did what any self-respecting academician would do: she designed a study! Numerous studies, in fact. The results of her research were first presented in 1994:

◆ Signing children have better recognition of letters and sounds than nonsigners. They are better spellers and have larger vocabularies.

◆ Children who sign speak better and have more advanced communication skills than nonsigners.

◆ Children who had been taught American Sign Language had higher reading levels than those who had no ASL instruction.

The results of Dr. Daniels's work have been published in her book *Dancing with Words: Signing for Hearing Children's Literacy* (see Appendix D). In addition to encouraging parents to sign with babies and children, she recommends that teachers incorporate ASL into their everyday curriculum. Educators who have followed her advice give the idea "rave reviews" and claim that children not only enjoy the experience but that sign language actually does accelerate literacy and learning.

Behind the Signs

Want another way to boost your baby's IQ? There is solid evidence that children develop higher intellectual ability if they receive love and a proper diet as babies, particularly if they're breastfed.

Exactly How *Your* Baby Will Benefit

Now you know why teaching your baby to sign is so important. Basically, it's a way to give him a head start in life. But the researchers forgot to mention that signing with your baby is also lots of fun! And, as you are about to see, that's only one of the side dishes being served with the main course. I've mentioned this before, but it bears repeating. The benefits that are mentioned in this section are based on the "average." Your baby may not do as well, or he may outperform them all.

Let me get back to the researchers for a minute. Didn't you find it a bit bothersome how truly impersonal those scientists could be? It was all about babies as "statistics" and babies as "test subjects." Well, it's a good thing that I take a more caring approach. What about *your* baby? How will *he* benefit from the experience? Okay, get ready. This time it's personal.

Emotional Benefits

There are countless gifts you can give your baby. But signing parents give their little ones something that not even Bill and Melinda Gates can buy—emotional well-being.

- ◆ **Less frustration.** When you give your baby a way to express his feelings, there is little or no reason for him to be frustrated. He'll discover that signing empowers him and that it's more productive than crying, whining, or throwing a fit. He now has the tools to communicate specific information to you.

- ◆ **Greater self-esteem and self-confidence.** Studies show that reaching out and being understood by a grown-up is important for any child. A signing baby grows up thinking well of himself because of the positive responses of everyone around him. Sure beats an inferiority complex.

- ◆ **A closer parent-infant bond.** When you sign with your baby you'll spend more time together. And we're talking "quality time" that's chock-full of positive interactions. You'll find that parenting is less custodial and reactive. And your baby will discover much sooner who's boss. (Guess who *that* might be?)

Behind the Signs

Signing babies can initiate "conversations." They can "tell" you that they saw a dog or an airplane and want you to pay attention to it. Parents say that they never realized how many airplanes flew overhead until they taught their babies that specific sign.

Social Benefits

Once your baby has an effective way to communicate, he'll play a more active role in the family and develop a closer bond with siblings and caregivers. He'll be able to make demands and get away with it. Everyone will think it's *soooo* cute! Then there's big bro and sis. They'll feel like VIPs teaching the little one new signs. And when the babysitter takes over, she'll be able to speak the baby's language and the baby can boss her around, too!

Language Benefits

When you sign with your baby, you spark his language ability, not dampen it. A baby's first sign stimulates his interest in two-way communication and motivates him to perfect his skills all the way to the spoken word.

Another relevant finding in the Acredolo-Goodwyn study was that boys use signs as much as girls do. When it comes to language development, boys are usually slower to speak. This evens the playing field between boys and girls, at least when it comes to signing. Girls still speak earlier than boys. Why is that? One theory that's gaining popularity is that mothers speak more to their daughters than to their sons!

- ◆ **Early communication.** Your baby has the ability to understand what you're saying long before his muscles enable him to respond. Once sign language bridges that gap, he won't have to wait to let you know that you're not living up to his expectations. He can start critiquing you—right now!

- ◆ **Earlier speech.** If you're worried that sign language will delay your baby's verbal language development, forget it. Just the opposite is true. It is a proven fact that babies who sign speak *earlier* than those who don't. Signing will not stifle your baby's verbal language development; it actually *helps* babies learn to talk. Don't listen to anyone who tells you differently. In this case, even ignore your own intuition.

- ◆ **Larger vocabulary.** By the time a signing baby reaches the toddler stage, he has about 50 more spoken words than a nonsigning tyke. At three, he'll speak and understand at a four-year-old level. But because we all know that *your* child's not average, who knows what and how much he'll be saying!

Cognitive Benefits

When you sign with your baby, you get a child who speaks earlier and is more emotionally secure ... and who is smarter than the kids who don't sign!

♦ **Greater brain function.** Research on the brain has uncovered some amazing facts. Here's one of them: spoken language is stored in the left side of the brain. Information obtained visually is stored in the right side. Because signing involves spoken language *and* eye involvement, both hemispheres of the brain are used. Simply put, signing will help build more of your baby's brain and greater brain function.

♦ **Higher IQ.** Of course, nothing can be 100 percent guaranteed, but research indicates that babies who sign have higher IQs than babies who don't. Researchers Acredolo and Goodwyn give them as much as a 12-point advantage. While creating a smarter baby shouldn't be the primary reason to sign with your baby, you can't ignore what researchers have found.

♦ **Higher reading level.** Because one way to reinforce the signs that you'll teach your baby is with books, your baby will look forward to using them more interactively. And speaking of books, research shows that signing children read at a higher level than nonsigners. If signing can boost literacy, how can you look the other way?

What's In It for Parents?

Of course all the benefits I've been discussing are reward enough for any loving parent. But isn't it amazing to think that there's personal payback for you, too? Talk about a win-win situation!

♦ You'll enjoy earlier and more meaningful interactions with your baby. Think how amazing and how much fun it'll be to see the world from his perspective.

♦ Your anxiety level will plummet. No need to guess where it hurts or what your baby wants when he's upset. His signs will provide you with specific information about what's going on. That will make the both of you feel better.

◆ You'll even have a brighter future! Face it. The "terrible twos" are inevitable. But fear not, they're not as terrifying for the signing parent! One of the causes of tantrums and other negative behavior such as biting or kicking is a child's inability to communicate. When he can't express himself, it can get ugly. *Your* child, however, will have the ability to sign and can revert to signing when words fail him. Just think how that will improve *your* life.

◆ Getting babysitters will be a snap! When you include grandparents and babysitters in the signing experience, they'll have an easier, more enjoyable time with your baby when you're not there. That means longer and more romantic nights on the town for you and your partner.

Behind the Signs

Today ASL is used by more than one million Americans. It has been accepted as a foreign or second language for high school students in California since 1987. College and high school students in over 40 states can now elect sign language as their foreign language.

◆ Experience more peace and quiet. There will be less crying in your household once your baby learns that signing gets better and faster results than his former routine.

◆ You'll have the knowledge that you have given your baby a gift that lasts a lifetime—and, if you're so inclined, a head-start in learning a second language: ASL.

Bragging About Your Bilingual Baby

The signs you will teach your baby are based on authentic ASL. While some baby sign language programs suggest that you make up your own signs or use a combination of homemade signs and ASL, your best bet is going with the real thing.

See if you agree with my reasoning. Even if you only use sign language as a way to communicate with your baby before he actually talks, why not use elements of a real language? Who knows, you may want to continue your baby's sign language education beyond his early years. Then you can brag to your friends about having a bilingual child. Of course there's a more practical reason to teach ASL to your baby. It's a standard language that others outside your family will be able to understand.

Decades of research tells us that the period during the first two years of a baby's life is the crucial time to expose her to a second language, be it ASL or a foreign language. As you will find throughout the book, I am always climbing on top of my soapbox to stress the fact that sign language is just a step on the journey to verbal communication. But the time to plan is now. Sign language is a great beginning toward learning English or Spanish, French, Farsi ....

The Least You Need to Know

- ◆ Teaching hearing babies to sign is not a new phenomenon. Researchers have been studying it for more than 20 years.

- ◆ Hearing babies who sign receive a host of emotional, social, language, and cognitive benefits.

- ◆ Research shows that children who sign also have academic advantages, including better literacy skills.

- ◆ Parents also receive personal benefits when they teach their baby to sign—like more peace and quiet.

- ◆ Because it's a standard language that many others will be able to understand, teaching your baby ASL is your best option.

Chapter 3

Why and How It Works

In This Chapter

- ◆ Marveling at how your baby's brain develops
- ◆ Learning why your role is vital to the process
- ◆ Discovering the connection between sign language and the brain
- ◆ Recognizing the signs that tell you your baby is ready
- ◆ Learning when you can expect results

If you're anything like me, you get in the car, turn on the ignition, and give absolutely no thought to how you make it from your house to the grocery store and back again. Some of us just take things for granted, I guess. We're trusting souls. We don't care why things work, just that they do.

But because I know that you may be more curious (and lots more skeptical) than I am, let's take a closer look at the idea of teaching your baby to sign and find out exactly why it *does* work. Reverting to the automotive comparison, this chapter will give you an opportunity to kick the tires and look under the hood before you fire up the engine and take that baby out on the open road.

Your Baby's Amazing Brain

Throughout the centuries the brain has been a riddle to scientists. The ancient Greeks were convinced that the *lungs* directed our thoughts, feelings, and emotions. And if you lived in the eighteenth century, "experts" would analyze your skull to find out what was going on in your brain. If you had large temples, you'd have a talent for music. And certain characteristics at the base of your skull told them whether or not you'd make a good parent.

Seems ridiculous, I know, but even today, some questions about the brain go unanswered. Modern techniques have, however, turned up some pretty amazing facts about the brain and, in particular, how it develops. What they've found puts an even greater responsibility on parents. Cutting to the chase: the experiences you give your baby during his first years have a *profound* influence on how his brain will develop and his future learning ability.

You Gotta Have Connections

When a baby is born he has about 100 billion nerve cells. According to neurologists, he won't grow any new ones—*ever*. If that's the case then, how does a baby's brain grow after birth? By increasing the number of connections (synapses) between the neurons within his brain.

Behind the Signs

A baby is biologically primed for learning. By age three, a child's brain has twice as many synapses as an adult's. When those connections are used repeatedly in the early years, they become permanent. If not, they don't survive.

Each neuron is like a tiny octopus with thousands of tentacles. They carry signals that allow us to hear, see, taste, feel, move, remember, and think. It's where a baby stores information. A baby arrives with a limited number of these responses already intact. He is only capable of hearing, feeling, sucking, and seeing in black and white. Yet within just a few days his brain begins to analyze the outside world. With every experience, with his or your every touch, with every single sound that he hears, another connection in his brain is made. The more the connections, the more the baby is capable of complex thinking.

That's Some Responsibility!

What does all this mean? Doesn't genetics count for anything any more—aren't Mom and Dad's genes responsible for current and future brain development? Not totally, say the experts. In fact it looks as if your genes only determine your baby's main circuitry, those that control basic functions like breathing, heartbeat, and reflexes. That means that trillions of connections will be determined by the stimulation that you give your child throughout his early years.

It's incredible information, don't you think? In a nutshell, researchers have found that nurture trumps nature. Yes, genetics is important, but it's not the only thing responsible for your baby's brainpower.

But it's also exciting, isn't it? To think that the more you offer your child in the way of sensory and educational experiences, the more powerful his brain will become? Not only will these experiences change the physical structure of your baby's brain but they will have a major impact on his intellectual and emotional well-being throughout his entire life.

Behind the Signs

During the first month of life, the number of connections, or synapses, dramatically increases from 50 trillion to 1 quadrillion. If an infant's body grew at a comparable rate, his weight would increase from 8.5 pounds at birth to 170 pounds at *one month old.*

Don't Panic!

So what's a parent to do? Some are racing out to corner the market on all the developmental DVDs that are out there. Not so fast! Current research is taking a second look as to how effective those products are. They can be entertaining, for sure, but can they build a better brain? Not without person-to-person interaction, it seems. That means that all the CDs and DVDs that claim to boost a baby's IQ only work when Mom and Dad get personally involved in presenting them. Would you like some better alternatives on ways to build your baby's brain? Thought you'd never ask!

- ◆ Read to your baby. ZAP! Connections are made in his brain.

- ◆ Sing to your baby. ZAP! You can almost hear them connect.

♦ Cuddle your baby. ZAP! More brain stimulation.

♦ Talk to your baby. ZAP!

♦ Add visual information at the same time that you're talking, and voilà! It's called *sign language!* ZAP! ZAP! ZAP!

The Sign Language Connection

Simply put, when you sign with your baby, you are building additional connections in his brain. You are providing him with information that is (or will be) meaningful, and you are repeating it and reinforcing the message. Every time you speak and sign with your baby—zap!— another brain connection is created. Exactly how does it work? How does sign language stimulate a baby's brain? Pay attention, class, while I take out my pointer.

The left hemisphere of the brain, located on the same side as your left hand, is stimulated by the words you say when you sign. The right side receives and stores the visual information (signs) that you present to your baby.

Take Note

When it comes to brain development, silence is far from golden. If a baby is rarely spoken to during his early years, he will likely have difficulty mastering language skills later in life. While a baby needs to hear as much language as possible during the first three years, it needs to be direct, personal communication. In other words, parking your baby in front of the TV is not a substitute, even if it's PBS.

Then there's the fact that your baby is doing something with his *hands*. That means that he's stimulating his brain with kinetic information and perfecting his fine motor skills at the same time. Simply put, signing with your baby is a multi-sensory experience—and a virtual bonanza for building more of his brain.

It's All in the Timing

There's another important thing that research tells us. It's true in many areas of our lives but especially so in the early stages of your baby's life. It's about the *timing*.

Given what you now know, it shouldn't come as a surprise that babies and young children learn more in their first five years than they will during the rest of their lives. Because most of the wiring or connections in the brain happen during that time, you only have a small window of opportunity to make a major impact. And here's something else you need to know. There are critical windows for developing a baby's potential within that larger five-year window.

A dramatic example is the window for visual development. If by around six months, a baby is not seeing the world around him normally, his vision will never be normal. Equal stimulation through *both* eyes is so important that if a baby with cataracts doesn't have them removed by six months, the risk for ongoing visual impairment or permanent blindness is extraordinarily high.

And then there's a baby's ability to learn language. The critical stage? Birth to age three. The more language that's presented to him during those years, the better his vocabulary and language skills will be throughout childhood and even into his adult life. Now, because experts tell us that parents who sign with their babies tend to talk to them more, your baby will be bombarded with aural stimuli in that area—another reason to sign.

When to Introduce Signs

When should you start teaching your baby sign language? As you will soon see, there are many variables—including when his brain is ready to figure it all out.

Most babies begin to make associations around six or seven months. That's when they start to understand that vocalizing gives them power. They make a sound and you come running. Once that happens, they begin to realize that signing is powerful, too—and that it's much more effective than crying.

A baby learns that when he cries, you'll appear on the scene but you may not give him what he wants, at least not immediately. When he signs, however, he discovers that he gets much better results. If he makes the sign for EAT, he gets a cracker. If he makes the sign for MORE, voilà—instant service!

But before any of that can happen, his cognitive skills must be developed enough to make the association between a certain sign and what it represents. He must also have enough memory to recall the signs and sufficient motor ability to produce them.

> **Smart Signs**
>
> In order for your baby's brain cells to grow and establish stronger connections, they must be exercised. Think of the sign language as one of the "barbells" that will help strengthen the synapses and neural circuitry of his brain.

Now I don't need to tell you that all babies are different. While seven months may be the average age that most babies are first ready to be exposed to signs, not all babies that age will be. Some will be at the starting gate at six months; others, not until 10 months to a year. How can you tell when the time is right for your future signer? Look for clues that he's interested in communicating:

♦ Does your baby look at your face intently when you speak?

♦ When your baby drops a toy or some other object, does he look to see where it went?

♦ Does your baby seem really curious? For example, is he turning his head to see what's going on around him?

♦ When your baby picks up an object, does he look to you quizzically as if he's asking for more information?

♦ Does your baby point to the objects that he wants?

♦ Is your baby already gesturing on his own? For example, is he reaching out to be picked up or waving "bye-bye"?

♦ Can your baby imitate gestures or actions?

If you answered "yes" to five out of seven questions, then it's time for you to get to work. If you answered "no" to the majority of the questions, wait a few weeks and review them again. Remember that babies are making major strides very quickly at this stage so a few weeks can make all the difference.

Manual Dexterity

Want another tip to help determine if your baby is nearing the signing stage? *Look at his hands.* Because a baby's hands must be agile enough to make the signs you are showing him, it's another factor you need to consider. While there are numerous resources available about a baby's developmental stages, there's hardly any focus on how a baby's hands develop.

2 months	A baby's hands start to unfold and briefly hold a rattle.
3 months	He plays with his hands and can hold onto the rattle a little longer.
4 months	He reaches for objects.
5 months	He grabs his toes. His reach is more accurate and he can transfer objects from one hand to the other.
6–9 months	He can pick up small objects with his thumb and finger. He reaches accurately. He can make a sign!
12–15 months	He can grip a crayon.

Jump-Starting the Process

If you've discovered that your baby isn't quite ready to begin, why not put the wait time to good use? Start learning the signs yourself, teach them to your family, and be ready when he is. Want an even better idea? Put your baby in training!

Here are some simple activities that will stimulate your baby's interest in sign language, improve his motor skills, and promote his verbal language development at the same time:

◆ Gently manipulate your baby's hands to help him with tasks that he's having trouble with.

◆ Place Cheerios on his tray one at a time.

◆ Clap to music and songs. Gently take your baby's hands and help him with the movements and gestures.

◆ Play sorting games. Yes, you will have to do most of the work but speak as you play and explain your reasoning to your baby throughout the activity.

◆ Take your baby to a mirror and play "Identification." Touch your nose and say, "This is Mommy's nose." Then touch your baby's nose and say, "This is Amanda's nose." Then move on to your mouth. You get the idea.

◆ Stimulate your baby with "touch and feel" activities. Present him with a number of different textures and let him feel the difference. For example, rub a silk scarf on his hand and then let him feel a scrub brush.

◆ Get out a bubble wand and help him move his arm to create bubbles.

◆ Encourage him to move an object from one hand to the other.

◆ Make good use of developmental toys with dials, cranks, buttons, and little doors.

Smart Signs

If you're not certain if your baby is ready to sign, go ahead and begin. Even if it's too early, the worst that will happen is that it will take you a bit longer to see results.

◆ Read to your baby as often as possible. Babies love repetition so limit the number of books that you read to him. Take his finger and help him point to the objects/characters while stressing the name of each.

◆ Play peek-a-boo. This simple activity is great for developing and maintaining eye contact. That's important when it comes to signing.

When to Expect Results

How soon until you see results? There are variables that you need to factor into the equation. It depends on how old your baby is and how regularly you sign with him, among other things.

While there are no crystal balls in this area, the following time-table will help to give you a general idea of what to expect and when to expect it. Again, let me stress that this is based on an *average* and doesn't apply in all cases.

3–6 months	While babies are too young to begin any serious signing, this is a good time for you to put your baby in training and jump-start the process. Plus it's a great time for you to practice what you're about to teach.
6–8 months	Your baby's memory skills are growing daily. If you begin signing when your baby is six to seven months old, you will probably see results about two months later. This is based on a high level of commitment and consistency.
8–10 months	Your baby's coordination skills have improved dramatically and he will be able to produce simple signs and begin to grasp their meaning. If you start at this stage, you should see results in six to eight weeks.
10–12 months	If you introduce signs to your baby at this age, you should see results in two to three weeks—even faster if you are using the express method (see Chapter 5).
12–18 months	This is a prime imitation period. Watch what you say and watch what you sign. It could be picked up instantly, although the realization of what you're doing and why you're doing it may take a few days to a week.

Signing Variables

Why can't I be more exact? It's common sense, really. There are just too many variables that need to be considered:

◆ **Your baby's age.** The older the baby, the faster he will sign. (Bet you couldn't have figured that out on your own.)

◆ **What else is on his mind.** If your baby is learning to crawl or walk, that could delay things for awhile. Babies under nine months are still trying to control their arms and legs. They will learn to sign eventually, but they can only do so much all at once. Cut 'em some slack!

◆ **Your baby's mood and interest level.** Your baby may not be interested in what you are teaching him. Try other signs. Or maybe he's just crabby that day.

◆ **Your level of commitment.** The more committed you are to the concept of signing, the faster your baby will begin.

◆ **Your consistency level.** The more you sign with the baby, the faster he will catch on.

◆ **The family's level of involvement.** The more that parents and other family members get involved, the quicker the results.

Rather than worry about *when* your baby will sign, try to have fun with the process. Until your baby shows you that first "sign" of progress, it may get a bit repetitive. But repetition is how your baby will learn. The problem with repetition, however, is that it's often accompanied by its nasty sidekick, boredom. And you simply cannot allow that monster to rear its ugly head!

Don't Give Up!

Dear Diane:

I have been signing with my Billy since he was eight months old. Now he's 11 months old and he's still not signing. I am so frustrated that I am about to give up!

Signed,

Frustrated in Frisco

Dear Frustrated:

Don't you dare! I know that not seeing immediate results can be discouraging, but the benefits for Billy are so remarkable that you can't afford to abandon the effort.

You probably just have a slow signer. One day, maybe even tomorrow, it will happen. When it does, it'll be like someone switched on a 300-watt light bulb over his head. It will be the moment when you (and he) realize that he gets it! He really, really gets it!!

One day soon you'll look at his chubby little hand. You'll see that it's heading for his mouth! Then he'll do it again and you'll realize that Billy wants to EAT.

Then he'll do it faster and maybe give you that impatient look of his. Hurry up, give him a cookie or something! Then he'll make another sign, the one for MORE. There's that impatient look, again. He wants MORE and he wants MORE—now!

The morale of the story? Be careful what you wish for.

P.S. Of course, I jest! You just can't take this thing too seriously. Billy will sign when he's ready. So relax, keep doing what you've been doing and enjoy what your baby is doing today!

Hang in there!

Diane

Now, did I really know why Billy wasn't signing? I hadn't a clue. As I said, there are far too many variables. It could be that he just didn't feel like it.

It's like the story of little Matthew. Normal birth. Normal weight. Normal development. Yet by the time Matthew was three, he hadn't said a word. Naturally, his parents were concerned. They took him to a pediatrician and everything checked out fine. There was just no physical reason why Matthew wasn't talking.

They took him to a speech therapist. She couldn't figure it out, either. Matthew celebrated his fourth birthday. And not a sound did he make.

And then it was time for Matthew to go to kindergarten. His mother woke him early so he would have a nice breakfast before boarding the school bus. She opened a box of cereal, a new brand, and put some in his bowl. Matthew took a bite.

All of a sudden, Matthew made a horrific face and spit the cereal on the floor, and exclaimed, "That tastes like miserable, stinking garbage! You have some nerve serving me something as disgusting as that!"

His parents were both thrilled and stunned! "Matthew, My God! You spoke! After all these years, you finally said something. Please tell us, why after all this time did you decide to speak?"

Matthew glared at them with his hands on his hips and said, "Up 'til now, everything's been fine."

So there you have it. The same holds true when it comes to signing. If your baby doesn't feel like it, if you don't give him a reason to sign, it's not gonna happen. You have to make it fun and you have to make it relevant. And some day, like Billy and Matthew, he'll get it. He'll really, really get it.

The Least You Need to Know

♦ A baby's brain is a work in progress. How smart he will be goes beyond genetics; it depends to an even greater degree on the varied experiences he gets between birth and five.

♦ Sign language stimulates both side of the brain and promotes greater brain function.

♦ There is no exact age to determine when your baby is ready to sign, but there are signs you can look for to determine if he's ready to begin.

♦ Results of your signing efforts depend on many variables including the baby's age and how often you sign with him.

Part 2

Ready, Set, Sign!

Now that you have a basic understanding of what's involved with teaching your baby to sign, it's almost time to take this show on the road. Have a case of opening-night jitters? That's understandable. After all, this is uncharted territory for you. But take my advice, relax and have fun. Signing with your baby should be as natural as speaking to him. You really can't make any mistakes. Even if you don't follow my advice to the letter, the worst thing that could happen is that it'll take your baby a little longer to catch on. In Part 2 you'll learn what to do to get started. You'll also discover that there are two methods you can use: the traditional approach and our new, faster-than-lightning express version. It's up to you to decide which one works best for you and complements your personality and lifestyle.

Chapter 4

Introducing Baby's First Signs

In This Chapter

- Deciding when to start
- Discovering the difference between iconic and abstract signs
- Finding out which signs to teach first
- Learning how to teach other important signs
- Looking for signs of progress
- Following the Ten Signing Commandments

Kudos to you for getting this far and making the right decision. You may have been skeptical at first, but you read the background, studied the research, and came to the conclusion that teaching your baby to sign was something too good to pass up.

So what are you waiting for? Wake up that lazy child and tell him that the school bell is about to ring! Well, maybe you should give him another hour in the sack. Because, first, you have to learn to teach him how.

Traditional vs. Express Method

Your first decision is to determine if you want to take the traditional or express approach. It really depends on your lifestyle and time constraints. Your baby will learn to sign regardless of which method you use.

The difference is in the timing. With the express program, which is described in Chapter 5, your baby should be 11 months or older and you'll need to put in an intensive two-week effort to see results at the end of those two weeks. The traditional method, which is described in this chapter, takes a more relaxed approach. You can start when your baby is as early as six months with results two to three months later.

Take a look at the express program in the next chapter. See if that sounds right for you and your family. Then you can make the decision to start at six months or wait until eleven months. Or you can start slowly now and, if you're not seeing results, you can always switch gears and move into the fast lane.

By the way, all of the techniques contained in this chapter also work for the express program, so feel free to use them regardless of which approach you are taking.

Sign Language Categories

Okay, I know you're anxious to get going, but you still need to stay in neutral for a few minutes more. There's a bit of technical information that you need to know before you're off and running. It may seem a bit bothersome now, but believe me, it'll make things go more smoothly down the road. It has to do with the two types of signs you'll teach your baby:

◆ **Iconic signs.** These are signs that mimic the action or the look of what you're trying to communicate. Iconic signs are the easiest for you to teach and for your baby to learn. Take the sign for TELEPHONE, for example. You already know how to make that iconic sign. It's just like you thought. Thumb to your ear, pinky finger to your mouth.

♦ **Abstract signs.** These signs are a little harder to teach because their meanings can't be conveyed by a simple gesture. To teach them you'll need to create an association so your baby will make the connection. It sounds more complicated than it is. You'll understand better in our first example, the sign for MORE.

The First Three Signs: MORE, EAT, and MILK

The first signs you'll teach are MORE, EAT, and MILK. They've been chosen because they're important concepts to your little one. In fact, in the earliest stages, they're pretty much all that he cares about. He wants something to eat, something to wash it down with, and more of both. Another reason they work well is that none of them look alike. They won't confuse your baby—or you.

MORE is the very first sign that your baby will learn. It's also the most important sign, as it will serve as the foundation for all others. Once your baby understands the concept of MORE and can make the sign (or even come close), the other signs will come quickly. For those reasons, I will spend more time on this sign and provide you with a greater number of examples. Of course, you are free to come up with your own. I've just listed some to get you started.

Important Note: If you're taking the traditional route, introduce MORE and stick with it until you see signs of progress. Then gradually introduce EAT and MILK when it makes sense to do so. Again, there are no rules. Some parents tell me they've introduced all three signs at once. That's fine, too, but it may take a little longer. It's totally your call.

The Sign for MORE

Even though it's an abstract concept, MORE is a sign that babies learn very quickly. Oftentimes it's their very first *spoken* word. It's also a good starter sign because there are many different opportunities to teach it throughout the day. In other words, *you* won't get bored.

Your baby can use this sign to ask for *more* food, *more* juice, or *more* pages of the book that you're reading to him. All he has to do is put the tips of his fingers together and "ask."

Put the tips of your fingers together a few times.

Behind the Signs

The average baby will eat 15 pounds of cereal in his first year. That's great news when you consider there's an opportunity to teach EAT and MORE with your baby's every spoonful.

Techniques to Teach MORE

1. When you're feeding your baby, give him a few teaspoons from that jar of green beans or whatever the "daily special" might be. Then stop cold. Before he can get upset, make the sign for MORE and ask, "MORE? Do you want MORE?"

   Continue this throughout the meal, making sure there are enough "feeding stoppages" so the idea begins to register. Repeat this pattern frequently throughout every meal, stressing the word MORE while you sign. Use an expressive and upbeat tone of voice. Smile and make a game of it. Eventually your baby will make the association if you keep repeating the routine. Like learning anything new, repetition is essential.

2. Grab a handful of Cheerios. While your baby's in his high chair, put one on his tray. When he picks it up and pops it in his mouth, ask/sign, "MORE?" Then quickly place another one in front of him. As soon as he eats it, be ready to have another one magically appear, remembering to reinforce the idea by signing and speaking every time.

3. Read a book to your baby. (Babies love to hear your voice and look at the pictures, no matter how young they are.) Stop at certain intervals, look at your baby, and ask/sign if he wants MORE. Repeat this several times throughout the reading session, always asking, "MORE? Do you want me to read MORE?"

4. Play Peek-a-Boo. It's always a baby-pleaser. Stop every so often and ask/sign MORE. Then resume playing the game. Then do it again and again. And again.

Take Note

When teaching MORE, be careful not to deprive your baby of food or anything else for too long a period. After all, you don't want to torment your child! Your goal is to get him to make the connection between the sign for MORE and actually getting more of something that he wants. Learning has to be fun!

5. Play Baby Toss-Up. All babies love it. Pick him up and toss him gently in the air and wait for the belly laughs to begin. Then stop and ask if he wants MORE. Repeat the activity.

6. Put a rubber ducky in his bathtub and sink it. Then have it pop up. If he thinks it's funny, ask if he would like MORE.

7. Gather around the kitchen table with your baby watching from his high chair or from someone's lap. Ask family members if they would like MORE of something. Exaggerate the effort. Have them respond (and sign) that they would. Then place MORE on their plates.

One idea that may help your baby make the connection is to recruit a favorite teddy or doll with moveable hands. Give Teddy a cracker, for example, pretend that he ate it, and then ask if he would like MORE. Then bring Teddy's hands together, making the sign. Make sure your baby is watching the action, of course.

The Sign for EAT

Move your hand back and forth to your mouth as if you're eating.

Our next sign is a simple one. It's the sign for EAT. To learn it, your baby will have to make another association. But because the sign for EAT pantomimes someone actually eating something (iconic), it's one that is easy to teach and easy for everyone to remember.

Behind the Signs

Did you know that 10 to 13 percent of the world's population is left-handed? So are 22 percent of all twins. Researchers say it's decided in the womb as early as 10 weeks. What's the connection? If it's a one-handed sign, it doesn't matter which hand you sign with. Right or left, just keep it consistent.

Techniques to Teach EAT

1. It's suppertime and your baby is in his high chair watching you prepare his food. You can tell by his behavior that he's excited about the prospect of eating. Sit down in front of him with a bowl of his favorite strained vegetables, and *before* you begin to feed him, ask/sign, "EAT? Would you like to EAT?" Again, your voice is upbeat and you are smiling. This has to be fun!

   By the way, did you notice the difference between EAT and MORE? With EAT you make the sign several times *before* feeding your baby. Why is that? It's common sense, really. If you stop and start throughout the meal to teach the sign, your baby will get EAT and MORE confused.

2. You don't have to wait until your baby is in the high chair to help him make the association. When you get him out of his crib and dressed before breakfast, make the sign for EAT *before* you leave the room, asking him if he is hungry and ready to EAT his cereal. Then make sure you take him *directly* to the high chair so he makes the connection. On your way there, ask/sign that same question a few more times. Remember to speak when you sign. No exceptions.

3. Surprise your baby at other times of the day by asking him if he would like something to EAT. Repeat the question a few times, and then produce a cracker so the meaning is reinforced.

4. Use whatever props you can think of to reinforce the sign and its association. For example, feed the dog or a family member, or offer a pretend-snack to a stuffed bear.

The Sign for MILK

When you introduce the sign for MILK, you have a different kind of association to make. MILK is something your baby can see and touch (a bottle or a breast).

Your hand opens and closes as if you were milking a cow. Alternative: Many nursing moms use the sign for NURSE. It's made by quickly brushing your hand over your breast in a downward motion.

Techniques to Teach MILK

1. *Before* you give your baby his bottle or your breast, you will ask/ sign, "MILK? Would you like some MILK?" Follow the same method as with the previous sign, repeating the question a few times. Then give him the bottle or breast.

2. Now you have another opportunity to help your baby make the association. *During* his feeding, while his attention is focused on you, reinforce the sign by asking/signing, "MILK? Do you like MILK?" While it may be difficult to feed your baby and sign at the same time, ask your spouse or other family member to sign and say MILK/NURSE while your baby is feeding, making sure the sign is made within your baby's sightline.

Take Note

A few weeks after you have introduced a sign to your baby, take your baby's hands and gently shape them to form the sign. Be careful not to force your baby to do this. Just do it occasionally, as a way of encouraging your baby to imitate you.

Teaching Other Important Signs

One of the reasons babies enjoy signing is that it helps them feel good about themselves. They begin to gain a sense of independence. At last they have some control over what's going on. Why, they can even provide you with specific information about how you're not measuring up! But only if they have the signs they need at their disposal, of course.

While I've already stated that you should adapt these guidelines to meet your own goals, would you mind if I made one *strong suggestion?* In the beginning stages, teach your baby the signs that he (and you) really need. In other words, teach him the following signs *before* you venture into the good manners and good grooming categories. You can always show him the sign for "toothbrush" next week.

The Sign for HURT/PAIN

Bring the tips of your index fingers together a few times.

The sign for HURT/PAIN is one of the most important signs you can teach your baby. Once he learns this sign, not only will he be able to tell you when he's in pain, but also where it hurts. Instead of simply crying, your baby will have a valuable tool to help him communicate the source of his pain. He'll simply make the sign at the place on his body where it hurts. The bad news is that in order to learn the sign for HURT/PAIN, your baby must make the association between the sign and pain itself. Unfortunately, he'll have many opportunities to learn firsthand when he's crawling and starting to walk.

It doesn't matter what word you use: *Hurt, Pain, Boo-Boo,* and *Owie* all work fine. Just remember that consistency is essential, so select one and stick with it.

Techniques to Teach HURT/PAIN

1. When your baby has stubbed his toe or bumped his head, give him some cuddles and comfort and, of course, make sure that it's only a superficial injury. Then while you're soothing him, make the sign for HURT/PAIN where it hurts. If he injures his knee, for example, make the sign in front of his knee, saying sympathetically, "Did you HURT yourself? Does it HURT? I'm sorry it HURTS." Remember to stress the word HURT each time, always signing at the point of injury.

2. If the injury is outside your baby's line of vision (e.g., nose or forehead), gently touch or rub the spot where he was hurt and then make the sign for HURT at that same location on your own body. Make sure, of course, that he's paying attention and not still totally focused on his pain. Repeat this several times, talking to him soothingly. Another alternative is to take him to a mirror so he can see you make the sign at his own nose or forehead. That will help him make a more personal connection.

3. Pretend to hurt yourself while your baby is watching. Bump your knee, for example, and then overreact by hopping around, gritting your teeth, while making the sign for HURT at your "injury."

   Another time, pretend to walk into a wall and hit your nose. Overdramatize the situation each time, signing and yelling

"HURT" as your baby watches from his ringside seat. By the way, all babies really enjoy this activity. The heartless little creatures get a real chuckle out of someone else's suffering.

4. Use a teddy bear as a "crash dummy" and have him injure his head or paw. Then make the sign where he was hurt and top it off with a colorful Band-Aid to reinforce the point.

The Sign for HELP

Pat your chest with your palms open a few times. (Note: This sign has been adapted from American Sign Language [ASL] to make it easier for a baby to produce. The authentic ASL sign is also included in our dictionary.)

HELP is another sign you'll want your baby to learn. Not only will it eliminate a considerable amount of crying and frustration on your baby's part, but some of your own as well. You won't have to guess what's wrong with him when he starts to cry. Is he hungry? Tired? Teething? No, he wants HELP!

Techniques to Teach HELP

1. Look for situations where your child may actually need help; for example, his older brother takes his toy or rattle. He starts to

whimper. You come over and ask/sign, "HELP? Do you want HELP?" Then do whatever needs doing to rectify the situation.

2. Watch your child at play. If you notice a situation where you think he may need help, go to him and ask/sign, "Do you want Mommy to HELP?" If he indicates in any way that he *doesn't*, then back off. Remember, you're not only trying to teach him sign language, but you also want him to learn independence.

3. Because situations where your baby needs help may not occur frequently enough for him to make the necessary association, you need to get creative again with some edu-tainment. Keep the plot simple, remembering that you are playing to an audience of one.

As with HURT/PAIN, it's important that your baby sees your little HELP vignettes played against different backdrops. You don't want to bore him with the same storyline week after week, do you? Once again, you will have to sacrifice your dignity for the greater good, but things are improving. At least you won't have to walk into any walls.

Ready for your close-up? Don't be shy, now. The more of a hambone you are, the faster your baby will learn. Get ready for what I like to call the "Academy Award" technique. ACTION!

"As the Bowl Crashes"

Starring: Mary Sunshine, her swashbuckling husband Rex, and their son Baby Boswell

Setting: An ordinary kitchen in Middle America. The family is gathered around the table. Baby Boswell is in his high chair taking in all the action.

Direction: Mary reaches for a bowl on a very high shelf and can't get it. She exaggerates her plight, signing as she cries for HELP!!!

Mary: Rex, can you HELP? I need HELP getting this bowl down from the shelf. Please come and HELP!! Oh, won't someone HELP?!!

Rex: Mary, did you say you needed HELP? I would be glad to HELP. Why didn't you call for HELP sooner?

Mary: Oh, Rex, you're such a big HELP—and my hero!

THE END

Here's another reason to vary these rescue scenes. If you repeat the above scenario too often, your baby is liable to make the sign for HELP when he wants a BOWL.

The Sign for DIAPER CHANGE

All fingers except the thumb curl into your palms. Your knuckles rest against each other and pivot in opposite directions. (Note: The sign for DIAPER CHANGE is actually the sign for CHANGE, with "diaper" implied.)

Can a baby really "tell" you when he needs his diaper changed? Yes, if he wants to. With today's disposable diapers, your baby might not feel uncomfortable or mind being wet or messy. Yet there are babies who *abhor* the feeling and would be thrilled to have a more efficient way to call for personal valet service.

Take Note

Some babies really hate having their diaper changed, so this sign may not be one of their favorites. In fact, if you ask/sign if they want a DIAPER CHANGE, some toddlers may run the other way. If that happens, don't waste your time with this sign. Babies will only learn the signs they're interested in.

DIAPER CHANGE is not as essential as the other signs, but because it may benefit your baby, why not give it a try and see what happens?

Techniques to Teach DIAPER CHANGE

When you introduce the sign for DIAPER CHANGE, your goal is to get your baby to communicate when he's uncomfortable and wants you to change his diaper. In order for your baby to make this association, he needs to be aware of the process of having his diaper taken off and on. Your reactions when you actually change his diaper will help to reinforce that awareness.

1. When a baby has a wet or soiled diaper, make a big deal about changing it. Because the sign requires two hands, put your baby on a blanket on the floor or some other safe place. Then say/sign, "DIAPER CHANGE? Do you want your DIAPER CHANGED?" Repeat this a few times, making sure you stress the words DIAPER CHANGE as well as the sign.

2. Remove your baby's diaper, all the while saying/signing something like "You really needed a DIAPER CHANGE!" or "A DIAPER CHANGE is my favorite thing to do."

3. Once the diaper is off and your baby is clean, let him go *au naturel* for a while, enabling him to feel the cool air on his bottom.

4. While he is still in the buff, play the "Diaper Game!" Place a diaper behind you or somewhere out of your baby's sight. Then say/sign, "Where is the DIAPER?" Pretend to look around you while asking the same question. Keep repeating it and signing. Then magically bring the diaper into your baby's sightline as you enthusiastically say/sign, "Here's the DIAPER! We found the DIAPER!"

You can also diaper a teddy bear or baby doll to help your baby make the association. In fact, using a "stand-in" (real or otherwise) works well in teaching many of the signs. In this case, don't ask for human volunteers. Family cooperation will only go so far.

While we are on this delicate subject, I should remind you that we will delve into it in much greater detail in Part 3. The sign for DIAPER CHANGE may not be essential for your baby to learn at this stage, but other signs will become invaluable when it's potty-training time.

Behind the Signs

According to behavioral experts, men are faster than women when it comes to changing diapers. Research shows that the average woman takes two minutes and five seconds. Men can take a diaper off (and put it back on) in one minute and 36 seconds! One expert says it's because men think of it like a mechanical process and want to get it over with as quickly as possible. (Like women *don't?*)

Looking for Signs of Progress

Okay, let's say that you have been signing for a month or two and nothing is happening. If you think that your baby should be making better progress (based on all the variables we discussed earlier), there are some things you can do to determine if you're making any headway.

1. Say a target word (MORE, EAT, etc.) *without* making the sign. Pay close attention to see if your baby's eyes travel down to your hands. If so, it means that he is used to receiving information verbally *and* visually. You are definitely making progress.

2. Give him another test. Place your baby's bottle on the floor with a few other objects. Then watch him carefully as you sign and say MILK. If he looks to the bottle, congratulations—you are really getting close. Try the same thing with a diaper, a book, or other object signs you are trying to teach.

3. Keep in mind that your idea of progress might not be the same as your baby's. His signs may not look like yours at first. It takes lots of dexterity to make some of them perfectly. In fact, your baby may already be signing and you may not even know it!

Recognizing Early Attempts

How will you be able to figure out what your baby is trying to sign to you in the beginning stages? No, his signs may not replicate yours exactly, but he *is* doing his best and should be rewarded for his efforts. So pay close attention!

Be on the lookout for any motions or gestures that seem out of the ordinary, especially if your baby keeps repeating them. If you still can't figure out what your baby is trying to communicate, look around you. Chances are it has something to do with the current situation or nearby object. Like any good detective, survey the scene.

If you're still stymied, it may help to know more about the first attempts of other babies:

- **MORE.** Some babies clap their hands together. Others close their fists and tap them together when they want MORE of something.

- **EAT.** There are babies who put their hand or fist in their mouth or point to their mouth with one finger when they want something to EAT.

- **MILK.** A thirsty baby may wave or shake his hand or even reach out toward your bottle or breast for MILK.

> **Smart Signs**
>
> When your baby approximates a sign, show him that you're pleased with the effort but then demonstrate the correct way to do it. Don't imitate his attempt. As your baby's fine motor skills improve, so will his ability to make the sign properly. Give him something to strive for!

Do what you can to identify what your baby is trying to communicate to you. Once you do, lavish him with praise while showing the correct sign as you say something like, "Yes, Tommy! You want MILK? Aren't you the smartest boy, telling Daddy that you want MILK? Now, can you sign SKIM or TWO PERCENT?"

The Ten Signing Commandments

Follow these do's and don'ts to keep you on the straight and narrow—and help you achieve signing success:

I. Always sign in context.

II. Once you begin to sign in a certain situation, continue.

III. Remember to speak as you sign.

IV. Use body language along with maximum facial and vocal expression.

 V. Encourage a reluctant child to sign by occasionally (and gently) shaping his hands.

VI. Reward your child's efforts—even if just comes close and approximates a sign. Cheer him on!

VII. Use any and all creative ways to reinforce signs.

VIII. Never show disappointment or express any negative reactions.

 IX. Have patience! Don't expect instant results.

 X. Make the sign language experience meaningful and fun!

The Least You Need to Know

- The first signs you will introduce to your baby are MORE, EAT, and MILK. MORE is the most important sign and the foundation for all other signs.

- In the traditional program, wait until your baby masters MORE before you introduce other signs.

- Depending on the age of your baby and your own personality, you have two options to choose from—traditional or express.

- HURT and HELP are important signs for your baby to learn.

- Your baby may not be interested in the sign for DIAPER CHANGE, but it's worth giving it a try.

- Be on the lookout for signs of progress. An unfamiliar gesture could be a first attempt at signing. And don't forget the Ten Signing Commandments!

Chapter 5

All Aboard the Baby Sign Language Express

In This Chapter

- ◆ Teaching your baby to sign in two weeks or less
- ◆ Learning why the 11-month mark is important
- ◆ Following quick and easy steps to reach your goal
- ◆ Introducing additional signs
- ◆ Deciding where to go next

Welcome aboard the Baby Sign Language Express, the fastest way to communicate with your hearing baby through sign language. Now, I know some of you jumped right to this chapter, ignoring all the hard work and research that came beforehand. No need to apologize. I can understand why you were so anxious to get here. Imagine, signing with your baby in two weeks! Pretty amazing, don't you think?

There are two major components you will need in order to be successful in this venture. One is a baby who's 11 months or older, and the other is two weeks you can devote to the project.

Now, I'm not asking you to shut yourself up inside your house with your baby for that the period of time, but you will have to make signing a primary focus in your household. Plus, you'll need the help of anyone else who comes in contact with your baby. Think of it as a sign language immersion program.

How is this possible? Well, teaching a baby sign language is pretty standard regardless of the approach. The difference is that the express program consolidates and accelerates the experience with additional awareness opportunities in a more concentrated period of time. Whew! That's a fancy way of saying that you're going to do lots more, in lots less time—with amazingly fast results.

How Fast Is Fast?

Generally speaking, if your baby is 11 months or older and you follow my two-week program, you will see results in two weeks or less. That's right. You may see results *before* you have completed the program. One mother wrote to tell me it took her 13-month-old daughter less than a week to make her first sign. I think that would be considered fast by anyone's definition.

Smart Signs

While signing with your baby is an incredible thing, it is a small baby step in the entire communication process. Because your final goal is to promote verbal language development, talk to your baby as much as possible—especially while signing.

By comparison, when you sign with your baby using the traditional method, which I discussed in Chapter 4, you start when the baby is as young as six or seven months and see results in about two months. As always, there are variables such as the age of the baby and your level of commitment and enthusiasm.

What's the Big Deal About 11 Months?

At 11 months most babies will be developmentally ready to appreciate signing and will grasp the concept more quickly. They also have enough manual dexterity to mimic the gestures and sufficient brain power to remember the signs. Will some babies have those skills earlier than 11 months? Yes. But I still recommend this program for those 11 months and older. As I said, I want you to see results fast.

Another reason why 11 months is such an important benchmark is that it's closer to the period when you and your baby will get the most out of sign language. Frustration due to limited communication skills reaches its peak between 12 and 24 months. When you give your baby the ability to communicate—even on a very basic level—you are giving him a vital tool to express himself.

There's one exception to the 11-month rule. Let's say that you started signing with your baby when he was six months and incorporated sign language into your daily routine. Now it's three months later and your baby is not "getting it." In that case, try the express method. It will speed things up. In other words, if you have been signing for at least three months and getting discouraged, try it. Remember, what I offer are guidelines that you should adapt to your own baby and lifestyle.

Why the Big Rush?

The number-one reason babies don't sign is because parents lose their enthusiasm and quit. Perhaps they started too early, expected too much too soon, or just didn't have the time or patience to follow through.

I've received countless e-mails from despairing parents claiming that they have been signing "forever" and asking when they would see results. Until now I've only been able to play the role of cheerleader and try to motivate them to stay in the game. Now I have something else to offer: a speedier alternative. Even better, I can retire my pom-poms.

Take Note

Regardless of which route you take, don't start too early. Sign at the recommended ages to keep your own motivational level high. It's all about the timing.

The point is that the express program was not designed primarily for babies. Babies were (and are) just fine with the slower route. This is for parents who are looking for more immediate results.

Are There Any Guarantees?

Be serious. Can I *guarantee* that your baby will sign in two weeks? No. But I can guarantee that if you stick with the program and do just as

I say, your baby will sign as fast as he can. After all, this isn't a race. I encourage you to enjoy the experience of teaching your baby to sign—and you will be thrilled when it actually happens.

Remember, one size does not fit all. Your baby will sign when he is ready. While you may follow my instructions to the letter, your baby will sign when it makes sense for him to do so. Every baby is different and these predictions are based on the average baby. But we all know *your* baby is far from average. He may start signing tomorrow!

Baby Sign Language Express Method: Step-by-Step

You have two weeks to do a lot of work and make the baby in your life a more active communicator in the family. That's your mission. To accomplish it, you need a strategy that is both meaningful and fun, one that fully immerses your baby in the sign language experience.

Step One: Circle the Calendar

Decide on a two-week period of time when you feel you can devote most of your energies to teaching your baby to sign. Double-check your calendar to make sure there are no other major commitments that require extensive planning or will take up a large chunk of your time. (This is also a good way to get out of participating in the bake sale or going to the Tupperware soirée.) Of course, there are everyday things that still have to occur, but it's important to keep your signing awareness level as high as possible. Whenever you spend time with your baby within that two-week period, you have to think "sign language."

Step Two: Do Your Homework

Rather than repeating what I've written elsewhere, I'm going to refer you to other chapters for helpful hints and advice. While you may not be interested in the history and science behind teaching a hearing baby to sign, Chapter 4 is mandatory. In the express method we are going to be using those same techniques, so it's vital information. So are the Ten

Signing Commandments at the end of that chapter. Think of them as success tips rather than orders from on high. One other suggestion: to keep your motivational level elevated, Chapter 2 discusses all the benefits of signing with your baby. Glance at it over the two-week period. It will keep you going.

Behind the Signs

Manual dexterity plays a key role in sign language. And having opposable thumbs makes hand movements even more precise. Most primates (humans, apes, and Old World monkeys) have opposable thumbs, but humans can move their thumbs farther across their hands than any other primate. Thought you might like to know.

Step Three: Do Some Handiwork

You don't need to wait until you've completed steps one and two to undertake this component of the plan. Start right now doing whatever you can to bring focus and attention to your fingers and hands. Your goal is to make your baby aware of his hands and realize what fun it is to have a matching pair.

Also, concentrate on your baby's fine motor skills using visual and tactile reinforcement. Let him see you do interesting or even crazy things with your hands. Then take junior's hands and see if you can get him to duplicate those activities. But remember, this has to be fun for your baby. Chances are he'll love the "games" and think of you as the best play date he's ever had. (Revisit Chapter 3 for other ways to jump-start the process.) Get creative and come up with games and activities that will get your baby to pay attention to his and your hands. Here are a few ideas:

- Dance, wave your hands above your head, and move your fingers.

- Hide your face behind open fingers. Open and close them to play peek-a-boo.

- Draw a little face on your thumbs and let your thumbs have a "conversation."

◆ Wave bye-bye every time someone leaves the house—or even leaves a room. Wave as a car passes. Gently take your baby's hand and help him wave if he's having trouble.

◆ Play music and clap loudly to the beat. Take your baby's hands and clap for him.

Step Four: Recruit Your Volunteers

Set up a meeting with siblings, grandparents, caregivers, and anyone else who comes into daily contact with your child. If they know little or nothing about signing, give them the benefit of your knowledge (and mine) and talk to them about how much this will benefit your baby and how important their participation is. Then explain what will happen and their vital role in the success of the two-week venture. This is especially important if there are older brothers and sisters in the family—the best teachers of them all. Big bro and sis will love being included and thrilled to teach your littlest one to sign. It makes them feel important and special.

Smart Signs

If your child spends time in daycare or with another caregiver, it's important that they are involved in the process. Keeping everyone informed and updated speeds progress and enables everyone to feel good about what they're doing.

Week One: Introducing the First Sign

The first sign you will teach is the sign for MORE. To make the sign, the fingertips of one hand come in contact with the fingertips of the other. Check out Chapter 4 for an illustration of how to make the sign.

MORE is an important sign—not only because it's the first one you will introduce, but because it's the sign that will trigger awareness that gestures have meaning. So don't think of it as teaching a sign, but rather teaching its association.

The general concept is to identify something that your baby really enjoys, then stop during the activity, and ask if he wants you to continue—always verbally stressing the *word* MORE. "MORE? Would you like MORE?" Repeat the question with the sign a few times during each activity. After you ask the question, wait a few seconds as if you are expecting a response. Then give him more of what he wants—before he gets angry or frustrated.

In order for your baby to "get it," vary the signing contexts. Don't just use MORE at mealtime; use it throughout the entire day in as many circumstances that you can think of. More books, more peek-a-boo, more silly games. Keep asking him if he wants MORE. Keep in mind that once you start signing in a particular situation, continue to do it. Repeat. Repeat. Repeat. Repetition is the key to enlightenment! Check out Chapter 4 for some ways to help your baby make the association. Get creative and find what your baby likes best.

Week Two: Staying Focused and On Track

You made it through the first week. I'm proud of you. You have been signing MORE to your baby and repeating the activities whenever possible. Your family members have been doing the same thing. Your babysitter has joined you in the effort. What do you do now? Relax. Take a deep breath. You had a great week, right? Everyone takes this subject so seriously. You can't really make a mistake as long as you have your baby's best interest at heart. And you wouldn't be reading this if you didn't. So relax and keep going. Success is only one hand signal away.

Be On the Lookout!

At the beginning of the second week, start paying closer attention to your baby. You will probably notice that he will be paying more attention to his hands and yours—and maybe playing with his own hands more often than he usually does. During this time he may also make his first sign—or attempt to test it out and see if anyone's paying attention.

It's important to be aware of the fact that your baby's initial attempts at making the sign for MORE may not be as perfect as your own. He may clap, touch one finger to his palm, or open and close his fingers.

Regardless of how your baby makes the sign, you should continue to produce it correctly. Do not adapt to his signing variations because they may change as time goes by. As he gets older, your baby's signing proficiency will improve.

> **Take Note**
>
> Signing activities should only occur when your baby is in a good mood and enjoying them. Forcing him to clap his hands when he wants to rub his sleepy eyes will get you nowhere and could very well sabotage your efforts.

Wait a minute! Here I am critiquing your baby's signing skills when he—and you—did something incredible. Your baby communicated with you! It doesn't matter *how* he signed, he signed! So get excited. Praise him. And pat yourself on the back. You have just taught your baby to sign!

When Your Baby Makes His First Sign

Many parents liken the day their baby makes his first sign to the day he said his first word or took his first step. It really is a thrill and something to record in his baby book. Once you enter the event, however, it's time to get back to work. But it will get a little easier. When a baby makes his first sign, the others usually follow more quickly.

But just because your baby has made the sign for MORE, you can't cross that one off your lesson plan. It needs to be continually reinforced. It's the "use it or lose it" theory. Use the sign as before in all the previous situations—and make sure when your baby signs for MORE, you give him more of what he wants. Remember that you are reinforcing the association as well as the sign.

While you're reinforcing MORE, you are also going to be teaching two signs now—EAT and MILK. (Skip to "Introducing Additional Signs" a little later in the chapter.)

No Sign of a Sign?

If you have yet to see progress, don't get discouraged. Your time will come. Believe me when I tell you that you *are* making progress even if your baby's hands are still stuck in his mouth. Remember that your baby's receptive abilities at this age far outshine his expressive skills.

That means he is listening. He is paying attention. And he is just trying to determine what the best time will be for him to make his signing debut. The sooner you realize it, the better—*you're* not the one in charge here!

What you need to do now is exactly what you have been doing. Keep reinforcing the sign for MORE as you have been—and consider incorporating the following attention-getters into your routine. Your baby may just need some variety in order for him to start signaling for attention.

♦ Vary the proximity of the sign. As long as you have eye-contact with the baby, you can vary the distance.

♦ Touch or pat your baby's hand before you make the sign.

♦ Gently shape your baby's hands to make the sign—but don't force him to do it.

Now here's some news you may find surprising. Even though your baby doesn't seem to have a clue as to what's going on, *after one week* move forward. That's right. Even though you may not have seen any visible progress, your baby is paying close attention—and he's ready to take in more than MORE. (Pun intended.) Now you will teach him EAT and MILK.

Smart Signs

You may find that your baby chooses to say the word instead of using the sign. By always using the word and sign together you are giving him the option. In these cases, you keep using the sign and repeating the word so that your baby can perfect his pronunciation.

Introducing Additional Signs

Regardless of whether your baby is signing or not, after one week of signing MORE, you are going to introduce two new signs, the signs for EAT and MILK. It's important that you don't confuse the baby by using all three signs at one time. Use common sense. For example, introduce EAT by showing him a cracker and asking if he wants to EAT. Repeat that a few times. After he wakes up from a nap, ask if he wants MILK and show him his bottle. Gradually bring all signs together when you can tell he is making the connections. And don't forget MORE! You still need to include that in your signing repertoire.

Introducing the Sign for EAT

Take a look at Chapter 4 for ways to proceed with this sign. It's simply moving your hand back and forth to your mouth as if you are eating something. Pay particular attention to the section about keeping the signs for MORE and EAT distinct. Sign EAT *before* you put your baby in the high chair. And never use the signs MORE and EAT together, as it will result in obvious confusion.

Also continue to use the sign for MORE in a wide variety of contexts—not just when you are feeding your baby. The reason is that your baby may confuse the sign for MORE with the sign EAT—or think it's the sign for the Cheerios you are using to entice him.

Introducing the Sign for MILK

Open and close your fist as if you are milking a cow. If you are breast-feeding and prefer to use that sign, brush your hand lightly over your breast in a downward motion.

While you should again refer to Chapter 4, you probably don't need too much explanation. By now, you realize that signing is a matter of presenting the sign in such a way that the association makes sense. With MILK you have a natural way to reinforce that association. Simply makes the sign several times as you are nursing or giving your baby his bottle.

Deciding Where to Go from Here

It's your baby and your call. You have a few options, though. You can stop once your baby masters all three signs. It isn't essential that you do more. But why stop now? At the very least, keep signing until his speech takes center stage. Plus, signing will definitely help lower his frustration level if you send him off to the sandbox equipped with a few signs. Some parents tell me that they've almost become addicted to signing. Once they start, it becomes second nature. It's brought them and their family closer and has given the baby a more active role.

Behind the Signs

While authentic American Sign Language (ASL) is used in this program, it is in its simplest form. The art of ASL is much more complex. Subtle and not-so-subtle movements of the hands create entire words, phrases, and sentences often faster than the spoken word.

Assessing the Situation

I've always found that the best way to make a decision is to make a list of pros and cons. If you do that yourself, my guess is that your list of positives will far outweigh any negatives. In fact, I predict there is nothing listed on the negative side. At this stage of the game it certainly can't be "Takes up too much time." If you did write that, think it through again. The fact is that you have already taught your baby to sign. He's already learned that gestures represent something—and he will learn other signs almost as fast as you can teach him. Here's another way to look at it: you're helping him to speak, aren't you? How much more time will it take to toss in a few signs?

What Else Is There to Learn?

In many ways, the curtain has just come up. Your baby knows the signs, but he doesn't yet realize the power that he has in his hands—quite literally. He is ready for a larger role so he can more fully convey his full range of emotions. There are so many other signs to learn: signs that he can combine, sentences he can make, thoughts he can convey, questions he can pose .... And what happens when he *does* speak? Will he drop his signs altogether? Will he sign and speak at the same time? And what about your role in the process? Chapter 8 answers those questions for you.

I've referred you to so many chapters that the easiest thing for you to do is to simply read the rest of the book. I know that many of you zoomed to this chapter and were intrigued by this faster way to sign with your baby, but the rest of the material will help you put things in context and give you a better overall perspective. Plus, there are many valuable tips, tactics, and techniques you can use to enhance what you have learned in this chapter, and more than 120 signs to choose from if you want to continue the signing experience. And then there's signing and potty-training. Trust me, it will really help.

Behind the Signs

Baby sign language consists of gestures that represent a word or a concept. In cases where a sign doesn't exist for a particular idea, more advanced signers will spell out a word letter by letter, using the ASL alphabet.

An Important Note for Parents-in-Waiting

I know that many of you have read this material and are thinking about waiting for your baby's 11-month birthday. If that's the case, don't just sit around watching the calendar. Put the time to good use. There are a number of things you can do to promote signing readiness as you count down to the big day:

♦ Read this book from cover to cover and get ready for signing day. Practice the signs you'll be introducing.

♦ Play the manual dexterity "games" that are in Chapter 3.

♦ Continue to read and talk to your child. That will not only help with signing but with verbal language development as well.

♦ Remember, you can always start using the traditional method if your baby is at least 6 months old.

The Least You Need to Know

♦ The express program is designed for babies 11 months and older. This accelerated program is for parents who are looking for a faster and more streamlined approach.

♦ To be successful, it is essential that sign language be your focus for two weeks.

♦ Everyone involved in your baby's life needs to be an active participant.

♦ With this method, a baby can make his first sign in two weeks or less.

Chapter 6

Increasing Your Baby's Sign Language Vocabulary

In This Chapter

- ◆ Learning to teach two helpful signs
- ◆ Doing some planning and setting some goals
- ◆ Exploring signing opportunities
- ◆ Discovering how to combine signs
- ◆ Learning how to sign in sentences

So far, so good? I told you it was going to be easier than you thought. In fact, if you've taught your baby all the signs in the previous chapter, you don't really have to go any further! Many parents are content with just providing the basic signs.

If you decide to stop now, you and your baby will still reap many of the rewards I talked about earlier. However, you'll miss out on even greater benefits and lots more fun. So don't be a quitter!

Hang in there! You've gotten through the hard part. From here on in, it's smooth sailing. And I'm here to guide you every step of the way.

Helpful Signs to Teach

Some signs are more important to parents and caregivers than they are to babies. DON'T TOUCH and GENTLE TOUCH are two of them.

DON'T TOUCH is a combination of the sign for NO and the sign for TOUCH. As you might imagine, once your baby begins to roam, it's a sign you'll use frequently. Will it help him to communicate his wants and needs? No, it won't. As a matter of fact, there's a good chance your baby would prefer that you didn't learn these signs at all!

So why teach them? Because you're a good parent, of course, and you want to keep your baby safe. Learning DON'T TOUCH, for instance, will help you add emphasis to your verbal instructions. As your little one gets older, it can also be one of your "secret signs." When you're in a high-end shop, for example, and he reaches for that Waterford vase, you can simply flash the sign and you won't have to reprimand him in public. (Just to be on the safe side, I'd grab the vase first and then make the sign.)

The Sign for DON'T TOUCH

DON'T TOUCH is a combination of NO and TOUCH. Your index and middle fingers snap to the thumb (NO), and then your middle finger taps the back of the other hand (TOUCH).

Techniques to Teach DON'T TOUCH

1. Just as with any other sign, your baby needs to make an association. When you see him touching something that he shouldn't, quickly grab his hand, make eye contact, and show him the sign while shaking your head and sternly saying "DON'T TOUCH."

   As I said earlier, this will not be your baby's favorite sign but it will help you keep him out of harm's way. Just remember the four components that are necessary to get your message across: the tone of your voice, your stern facial expression, your spoken words, and the sign itself.

2. Play "The Untouchables Game." You can begin teaching this sign to your baby the fun way and then get serious later on.

   Spread some objects in a row on the floor. Five or six will do. It doesn't matter what they are, but one should be different in some way from the rest. For example, line up some of your baby's picture books and one of your own thick bestsellers. Or try five stuffed toys and one wooden one.

 Smart Signs

When you're teaching a sign, use every tool you can think of to help your baby make an association. Voice and body language should be at the top of the list. The look on your face, the tone of your voice, and your general demeanor will help to convey vital information.

Then touch each object, saying with a happy voice and a smile "Touch. Touch. Touch. Touch. Touch." When you get to the hardcover book, begin to touch it but quickly pull your hand away. At the same time, make a noticeable frown and say in a much deeper voice, "DON'T TOUCH!" and make the sign. Vary the sequence so the "untouchable" object isn't always at the end. After you do this a few times, take your baby's hand and gently guide him through the same activity.

If you play this "game" enough, your baby will make the association, plus he'll think it's an absolute riot—until you play it for real. Sure, it's a bit underhanded, but remember that it's for your baby's safety.

3. Another idea is to walk your baby around the kitchen touching different things while happily saying, "Touch. Touch. Touch." When you get to the stove or toaster, begin to reach out to touch them, then quickly pull your hand away, lower your voice, make a stern face, and say/sign "DON'T TOUCH!" This activity should be "played" more seriously than the previous version using the books or toys, as these are objects that you *really* don't want him to touch.

The Sign for GENTLE TOUCH

One hands gently "pets" the back of the other hand.

Another valuable sign is GENTLE TOUCH. Basically, it's one hand "petting" the back of the other hand, as if you were stroking a cat. And, speaking of cats, that's one of the reasons this sign is important. If you have a cat or other pet in your home or are visiting a friend who has one, your baby's first inclination may be to grab or squeeze it. With the GENTLE TOUCH sign, you can teach him to be kind and gentle in his manner of touch. The soothing tone of your voice as you "pet" your hand will help convey its meaning. The sign is also useful when holding delicate objects or when visiting friends with younger babies than yours.

Techniques to Teach GENTLE TOUCH

1. Touch your baby, rubbing his arm or leg while saying slowly and soothingly, "GENTLE TOUCH. GENTLE TOUCH."

2. Get out the props. Use a teddy bear or draft a live family volunteer. While your baby is watching, rub the subject's arm while speaking and signing, "GENTLE TOUCH."

3. If you have a family pet, pet him gently, guiding your baby's hand over his fur while saying and signing, "GENTLE TOUCH."

> **Take Note**
>
> Even if you choose not to introduce some signs to your baby, he may still pick them up by "osmosis." For example, don't be surprised one day when you tell your baby to do something and he looks at you and signs, "NO!"

Where Do You Go from Here?

Okay, time for a breather. You've worked hard and learned a lot in a very short time. Some of you may have already put that knowledge to the test and have started to sign with your baby. Others are scrutinizing their little ones looking for signs that they're ready to begin. And for those of you who are waiting for the stork to land, you couldn't have picked a better time to learn. Things are about to get a bit more hectic in your household.

No matter where you are in the process, I'm glad that you're sticking with me. But before you determine what the next step will be, you need to ask yourself what you're trying to accomplish—and set some goals. First, think long-term.

Do you want your baby to become skilled in sign language and use it into early childhood, maybe even as an adult? If that's your goal, keep in mind that this is *baby* sign language and it's as basic as it gets. It's a way for a child to communicate what he wants and feels in a very limited way. While this is a great place to start, if you are really serious about teaching sign language as a second language, a more comprehensive and structured approach is necessary.

If, however, you're like most parents and want to use sign language solely as a communication bridge before your baby can express himself with words, you need to decide which signs to teach after you've introduced the basics. No one can do it for you. After all, would you want someone to tell you what words your baby should say? Well, no one should tell you what *signs* to teach, either.

To help you establish your signing goals, ask yourself which signs would be most helpful to your baby in expressing himself. Also ask what would be helpful to you in understanding what he wants or feels. And don't forget the fun factor! Think about what signs your baby could learn just for the sheer delight of it.

Behind the Signs

Most parents consider baby sign language as an interim method of communication and teach between 10 and 20 signs. How long you sign with your baby and how many signs you teach are up to you. Research shows that even a limited exposure to sign language will benefit your baby.

To help you decide, look at the signs in this book's Baby Sign Language Dictionary. They are authentic American Sign Language (ASL) signs and are the most popular with parents because they are all relevant to a baby's world. Review the different categories and decide which ones you'd like your baby to learn. Family signs, perhaps? That would be helpful. Good manners? A good choice. Animal signs? Always crowd-pleasers. Regardless of your decision, keep in mind that the goals you set are simply *guidelines* to help you establish some direction. Keep them flexible. You'll soon learn why.

Introducing Additional Signs

If you're ready to move ahead, it means that your baby has mastered the basics. He's come to realize that gestures have meaning. He knows that when he makes a particular sign, he gets something he wants. By now, you've reviewed all the signs and have decided which signs you want to add to your baby's signing vocabulary. But *how* and *when* do you teach him?

Let me answer that question with another question: how would you go about introducing new *spoken* words to your child's vocabulary?

Hmmm. Hard to put into words, isn't it? That's because teaching your baby to speak is something that *just comes naturally*. You talk, your baby listens, and he imitates what he hears. If your baby sees something that he's interested in, he'll stare at it, pick it up, or point to it. You react by slowly saying the name of whatever he's interested in and by repeating the word so he remembers it.

Well, teaching your baby new signs isn't that different, really. The only difference is that when you say the word, you now add a sign. All it takes is a little preplanning, some common sense, and a keen eye.

Identifying Signing Opportunities

Let's say that you've decided to teach your baby all the signs in the clothing category. Keeping in mind that he must make an association before he can learn any of them, when do you think the ideal time would be to teach him? Bingo! Of course, it's when you're getting him dressed in the morning and undressed at night. Going for a walk outside? Teach him the signs for HAT and COAT.

 Take Note

Babies love repetition. It not only makes them feel comfortable when they're able to predict outcomes, but it also makes them feel more in control. The problem is that while babies *love* repetition, adults don't. So try to vary the signing routines and come up with different ways to help your baby make the necessary associations. You can't afford to get bored!

Interested in teaching your baby good manners? Mealtime would be a good place to start. What about animal signs? Use his favorite animal picture book. Analyze your daily routine. You're sure to discover many teaching opportunities right in front of you.

The important thing to remember is to make your teaching relevant. Always *sign in context*. It's critical that your baby associate some real meaning to the signs you are showing him. And because he won't figure it all out immediately, you need to make the signs and reinforce the associations repeatedly.

Creating Your Own Opportunities

There is a major resource available to you when it comes to introducing and reinforcing signs you want your baby to learn. It's something that's jam-packed with ongoing teaching opportunities. It's called *life*.

Look around you. Life is a signing classroom. Take your "student" on a few field trips. Even your backyard is an adventure to a baby. Just open the door and point to what you see, say the word and make the sign. What about a trip to the zoo? What a great opportunity to teach animal signs! And what better way to teach family member signs than hauling out the family photo album?

Following Your Baby's Lead

Another way (and the very best way) to figure out what signs to teach your baby is to *take the lead from him*. Yes, your baby can and will tell you what he wants to learn, if you pay attention.

Remember those goals I helped you set a few paragraphs ago and my advice to keep them flexible? I made that suggestion because your baby may have a different signing philosophy than you do.

Let's say, for example, you're sitting on a blanket in the backyard trying to teach your baby the sign for BOOK. All of a sudden, he throws down the book, looks up, and points to a BIRD. If that happens, it's a priceless opportunity to teach him a sign! In effect he's saying, "I'm not at all intrigued by that silly book. But I *am* really interested in that thing up there. What is it? Can you give me more information?"

What should you do when that happens? You have two choices:

1. You can say, "Sorry. This is inconsistent with the goals that I have established for you to reach today. Animal signs are one week from Tuesday."

2. You can keep your goals flexible, seize the moment, and say, "Oh, a BIRD (sign)! Look at that beautiful BIRD. Look, there's another BIRD."

Of course, you'll choose number two. It's common sense and good salesmanship. It reminds me of a recent trip I made to Morocco, when the merchant in a gift shop followed my every eye movement. When I glanced at a brass plate, he presented it to me before I uttered a single word. Wouldn't it have been foolish of him to bring me a stuffed camel when I was coveting a plate? (I wound up buying both, but that's beside the point.)

Being Prepared

To promote baby-driven signing opportunities like the one I just mentioned, *let your child explore.* Be prepared with as many signs as you can ahead of time. If he picks up a diaper, be ready with the sign for DIAPER CHANGE. If he picks up a sneaker, present him with the sign for SHOE. If he points to the TELEPHONE, your baby wants to know more about it. (Or else he wants you to order a pizza.) Give him more information! Tell him the name of the object and show him the sign.

As you can see, it's really helpful to know specific signs ahead of time. Review the signs in the middle of this book and practice those that are likely to come up. Because many of the signs are iconic—meaning they mimic the action or the look of what you're trying to communicate— you'll have an easy time remembering them. Learn a few more each day and you'll be an expert in no time.

But what happens if your baby picks something up and you don't know the sign? Don't panic! While it would be a shame to miss out on a signing opportunity, there will be other chances. Just remember to look up that sign and be ready the next time.

> **Smart Signs**
>
> How quickly you introduce new signs depends on your baby. Introduce one or two new signs and see how fast he catches on. Once your baby figures out that by making gestures his life will get easier, he'll soak up new signs like a sponge. Even if you give him more than he can handle, he'll eventually figure it out.

But, in the interest of full disclosure, there is another school of thought as to what you should do if you don't know a sign: *make one up.*

Remember the *Baby Signs* program I talked about in Chapter 1? In it, Professors Acredolo and Goodwyn suggest that you invent your own sign in a situation like that. Their advice is to create a simple gesture that represents the look or idea of the object. For example, if you don't know the sign for DOG, consider panting like one.

Whether or not you should follow that strategy depends on your overall objective. If you want your baby to take ASL seriously, then pass up the opportunity, look up the legitimate ASL sign, and be ready the next time. If your objective is shorter-term and you don't plan on teaching your baby any more signs after he learns to talk, then you might give it a try. *It's important to remember,* however, that others may not be able to identify the signs you created on your own because they're not part of any standard sign language. If it were me, I'd stick with ASL.

Your Baby's Own Inventions

In Chapter 1, you learned how Linda Acredolo became inspired to study this subject in the first place. If you recall, it was when her daughter Kate spontaneously began to make up her own signs. Her sign for FISH was to blow because there was a fish mobile over her crib and her mom had to blow on it to make it move. To Kate, sniffing and wiggling her nose meant FLOWER because she saw people doing something similar when they picked one from the garden.

So what do you do if your baby makes up his own sign? Babies are very smart and creative, you know, and it's possible that yours may create a sign that's not in the dictionary. What to do? Well, you could ignore his effort and pretend you didn't notice. Not a great idea, right? Or you could get excited, praise him for his creativity and respond by giving him what he wants or show that you understand in some other way. Sound like a better plan? I agree.

But then you have to make another decision. Do you incorporate your baby's invented sign into your sign language lexicon, or do you respond by showing him the actual sign that you want him to learn? When you think about it, it's pretty much the same quandary you had when your baby asked you for a sign and you didn't know it. Again, it's really your call and depends on how much of an ASL purist you are and want your child to become.

There's one really important thing you need to keep in mind if you do opt to continue to use your baby's own signs. Be sure to record it somewhere and let your family and other caregivers know about it. Nothing will dampen your baby's enthusiasm for signing like not being understood by everyone.

Pacing Yourself

How fast do you introduce new signs? Why not find the person in charge and get his input? Guess who that might be? Right. The one in the crib.

Again look to your baby for guidance. See if he's interested. If he's not, try again at another time. Just don't bombard him with too much information all at once. As a parent, you'll be able to figure it out. Trust your instincts. No one can read him like you can.

If your baby "asks" for a word/sign by looking or pointing at something, tell him what it is and, if it's relevant, show him the sign. If another opportunity presents itself, go for it. Keep using the signs that your baby already knows so they stay fresh in his memory, and then introduce new ones when it feels like it's the right thing to do. Keep it fun and keep it natural.

Behind the Signs

Whenever you offer a new word/sign to your baby, it makes another connection within the brain. Words are stored on the left side of the brain, and visual information (signs) is stored on the right side. The more you speak and sign to your baby, the more his brain is stimulated.

I've said this before, but it bears repeating: teach sign language the same way you teach your baby to speak. You're not concerned about *talking* to your baby too much, are you? Does he understand every single word that you say to him? Of course not, but that doesn't stop you from talking. In fact, the more you talk, the better his vocabulary will become. It's the same with signing. Your baby has an amazing brain. He will eventually sort it all out.

Combining Signs

While putting more than one sign together isn't essential to your baby's signing success, if you want him to matriculate to the advanced class, by all means, give it a try. Again use the common-sense approach. Do I really need to tell you, for example, not to combine two signs when your baby hasn't mastered one?

Sometimes your baby may make combinations on his own. Maybe he'll sign MORE and MILK when he wants a refill. Be prepared and be impressed when that happens!

If he doesn't combine signs on his own initiative, offer some encouragement. EAT and MORE would be a good starting combo. Just be certain that your baby understands *both* signs and *both* concepts. Common sense, again. Then follow the same techniques you used when introducing other signs, keeping in mind that repetition plus consistency equals success.

By the time a baby reaches the stage when he's combining signs, he should be saying at least a few words. Make sure your efforts are now even more focused on his verbal development. Use signs as a secondary means of support and motivation.

Signing in Sentences

There's another way of looking at signing combinations. You might even think of them as baby *sentences!* When a baby signs DOG and BALL, he's really saying, "The dog has a ball." If he signs EAT and ALL DONE, he is telling you that he can't eat another bite. While he obviously has a long way to go before he can embark on a career in the

Senate, these combinations represent a major stride in the way a baby is thinking. Putting two concepts together is a big deal for any baby. So lavish him with praise and cheer him on!

Take Note

Don't panic or express disappointment if your baby doesn't sign in a particular situation when he may have signed in that same situation before. He may simply not be in the mood. You don't always feel like talking, do you? Try to motivate him with a happy face and a few signing repetitions. If nothing happens, there's always tomorrow.

By the way, don't expect any signing combinations much before 18 months and maybe much later. They almost always happen when a baby should be speaking. That's why many babies use a combination of the two, making a sign and saying a word.

Your Little Conversationalist

In his book *Sign with Your Baby* (see Appendix D), Joseph Garcia talks about a time when one of his sons actually started a conversation by making a sign. According to Garcia, he and his sons had seen a few airplanes the day before and had fun making the sign whenever they saw one. A few days later while in his high chair, one son started making the AIRPLANE sign. Garcia was puzzled, as there were obviously no airplanes landing in the kitchen. And then it dawned on him. His son was recalling the experience from the day before and simply wanted to talk about it.

Was Garcia's belief based on reality or just wishful thinking? Was the baby actually initiating a conversation or was he just having fun with his hands? Who knows for sure, but because the possibility does exist, why ignore it? If your baby makes a sign out of context, take the cue and start talking about airplanes or whatever else he's signing about.

You might try something like, "Yes, I remember those airplanes. Weren't they big and beautiful?" Then if you can, find a picture of an airplane to reinforce the idea and sign at the same time. At the very least, these kinds of interactions help stimulate your baby's verbal language ability and will bring you closer together. And who knows, it could be step one toward your baby's talk show career.

The Least You Need to Know

- While they may not be your baby's favorites, DON'T TOUCH and GENTLE TOUCH are important signs to teach.

- When it comes to setting your goals, it's important to decide how proficient in sign language you want your child to become.

- To decide what additional signs you want to teach, pay close attention to your baby and see what he's interested in.

- Trust your instincts when it comes to adding new signs to your baby's vocabulary.

- While combining signs isn't essential, your baby may do so on his own to help clarify his message.

- When babies get to the stage when they are combining signs, they should also be speaking.

Chapter 7

Staying the Course

In This Chapter

- ◆ Learning how to stay motivated
- ◆ Incorporating sign language into your everyday routine
- ◆ Getting help and support from family and friends
- ◆ Dealing effectively with naysayers
- ◆ Staying on track with do's and don'ts

You've come a long way, baby. You, too, Mom and Dad. In fact, by the time you've reached this chapter, there's not much left that I can teach you. You have a solid grasp of what's involved and what you have to do to make it happen.

My guess is that at this stage you feel one of two ways. You're either chomping at the bit and can't wait for your baby to reach the signing stage (if he's not already there), or you're a bit overwhelmed by it all and are having second thoughts about the whole thing. (Collective gasp!)

Rid yourself of all doubt! Of course you're going to do this! You're planning on teaching your baby to *talk*, aren't you? Well, teaching your baby to sign is just like teaching him to speak—except you're going to throw in a few visuals (signs) to add emphasis to what you're teaching.

Staying Motivated

What's the number-one reason why babies don't sign? Their parents lost their motivation and stopped. Now I *will* admit that it does takes patience and commitment to teach sign language to your baby. And, yes, it's true that you could go months waving your hands in the air without any reaction or feedback from your little one. But trust me when I tell you that *it will happen*.

So stop second-guessing yourself. If you've been following the guidelines, success is in your future. Don't compare your progress with anyone else's. Just think positively and move forward.

Uh-oh. That's it, isn't it? You talked to your cousin Shelley and heard all about how *her* baby signed at nine months. So now you think you must be doing everything wrong and that you're a total failure because *your* baby is a year old and nothing is happening. Ready for the pep talk?

You're not doing anything wrong, and you are far from being a failure! Do you know what you are? You're a wonderful parent who is doing a fantastic thing by giving your baby an extraordinary gift.

And why in the name of all that is holy are you listening to your cousin Shelley? You never liked her anyhow. Plus, isn't she the one who's the lousy cook? Hey, that's it! Maybe her baby isn't signing at all! He could just be trying to cover his mouth so he doesn't have to eat her home-made baby food!

Okay, so what if her baby *is* signing? It has nothing to do with you. Your baby will sign, too—when he is ready. And when that day comes, all your efforts will have paid off big-time and you'll wonder why you ever had the slightest inkling of a doubt.

Let me reiterate: until your baby starts to sign, avoid asking other moms and dads about their baby's signing progress. Comparisons will only cause you needless concern. All babies have different developmental timetables and will crawl, walk, sign, and talk when they are ready.

Plus, here's a reminder in case you need one. If you are really to the point of abandoning your efforts, then you need to think about the express program. After all, I designed it for people like you!

If you have been signing with your baby and started after six months and feel that you should be seeing more results than you are, you should try the express method. It's simple and easy, and you can read all about it in Chapter 5.

So to those of you whose enthusiasm may be starting to wane, here's a sage piece of advice that my mother handed down to me. She learned it from her mother before her. Get over it! You've come too far to stop now. Just take a good look at your beautiful baby and think of what he'll miss out on if you do. Who, me? Laying a guilt trip on you? No doubt about it. I'm shameless when it comes to this subject.

> **Take Note**
>
> The primary reason babies don't learn to sign is that their parents give up. While signing may get repetitive until you first see results, push forward and keep your motivational level high. Boredom and complacency are hazardous to your baby's signing success!

Motivational Tips and Tactics

I have to be honest. Signing at first can be a bit repetitive. But keep in mind that it's only a short-term situation, one that will vanish the moment your baby makes his first sign. When that happens, you won't be able to stop yourself from grabbing your camera to record the moment for posterity. Your enthusiasm will be rekindled and you'll be proud of what you've accomplished, as you should be. So hang in there and keep your eyes on the prize. It's better than winning the lottery.

But while you're waiting for the big day, here are some tips that may help you keep the faith:

◆ Try focusing on the actual process of communicating with your baby and not just on the outcome. Appreciate the fact that you have such a wonderful treasure and be thankful for what he is doing *today*.

◆ Reenergize yourself by rereading Chapter 2 on the benefits for you and your baby.

◆ Don't think of this as an educational exercise. Think of it as entertainment or as a challenge. Whatever works to keep you going.

◆ Ignore other people's comments about why it's not working, what you're doing wrong, or how they were more successful.

◆ Don't start too early. If you just brought your baby home from the hospital, you have about a six- to seven-month wait before you should even begin. Start signing when you're likely to get more immediate feedback.

◆ Keep signing in the same situations. Once it gets to be habitual, you may not even realize you're signing until one day, when you least expect it, those little hands will start flying. And so will you.

◆ Share your experiences and frustrations with others in the same boat. There are online groups for parents who are at various stages in the signing process (see Appendix D). Some parents have just started or are about to. Others are "old-timers," having been at it for months! Join in the experience and ask a question, share your thoughts and know-how, brag about your baby, and have a laugh with parents from all over the world. But remember, no two babies are alike, and hard as it might be, use their success stories as inspirations—not as comparisons!

Finding the Time for All of This

If one of the reasons you're feeling a bit uneasy has to do with time constraints, perhaps my response to an e-mail from an overworked mom in Colorado will help:

Dear Diane:

Thanks for all your hard work in helping us learn how to sign with our baby. I have read everything and you made it all very clear. The problem is that I don't think I can find the time to do it. We have two older children and they need our attention, too. Plus I have volunteer work and my husband travels quite a bit. And learning an entire sign language? Well, I just wish we had the time.

Signed,

Disappointed in Denver

Dear Disappointed:

Hey, Denver! Join the club! You are certainly not alone. Everyone's busy. We're all overscheduled with play dates, soccer games, cooking, cleaning, and maybe even trying to keep up with a career, but that's still no excuse. You're looking for a pass? Well, you're not gonna get one from me. I know I sound harsh and unsympathetic, but this is far too important for you to abandon!

Plus, who said you had to learn an entire sign language? You said that my instructions were clear? Apparently not clear enough. Here are some things you need to think about, girlfriend:

1. No one expects you to be a sign language expert. You only need to know a few basic signs.

2. You can teach as few or as many signs as you want. The number of signs you teach is not nearly as critical as the quality of the interactions you have with your baby.

3. Even if you just teach a few basic signs, your baby will benefit. If you find the time to teach him more, go for it.

4. Of course you shouldn't ignore your older children. Get them involved in this, too. They will love it!

5. Please know that you don't have to turn your world upside down in order to be successful. Work signing into your everyday routine. Do what you can. You'll find that it's easier than you thought.

I hope that helps. Write back if you need another dose of my motivational medicine. Good luck!

Diane Ryan

Cheerleader in Charge

Behind the Signs

While baby sign language has taken the world by storm, it's most popular in the United States and England. Check out the list of groups in Appendix D. They are great resources to ask questions, share the excitement, and maintain your commitment. Plus you may meet someone from the other side of the world!

A Day in the Life of Baby Signing Parents

If you're in need of a personal time-management coach, consider the job filled. While I can't offer one-on-one consultation, let me try to help you with some examples.

Wondering how you can integrate baby sign language with your own real world? Let's join the Jones family and see how they're managing it:

7:00 A.M. Baby's up! Everyone's up! Time to head for the nursery and watch little Belinda's face light up when she sees you. It's also time for her DIAPER CHANGE, followed by the question she's been waiting to hear, "Are you hungry? Ready to EAT?"

7:15 A.M. Whew! She really *was* hungry. Look at that empty bowl. ALL GONE. But maybe she wants MORE?

7:30 A.M. Hey, look who's making an entrance. It's DADDY! I LOVE YOU, too, DAD!

8:00 A.M. Time to get dressed. Those new SHOES fit perfectly. And what cool SOCKS! Hey, where are you going with my HAT, DOGGIE?

8:15 A.M. Early appointment with the pediatrician. Belinda sure hates needles, but she loves to ride in that CAR.

10:00 A.M. Snack time. CRACKERS, JUICE, and MORE of both.

10:30 A.M. A stop in the park on the way home to see the FLOWERS and BIRDS.

12:00 P.M. Lunchtime! EAT. MORE. MILK. BANANA. ALL GONE.

12:30 P.M. There's that lazy cat. GENTLE TOUCH.

1:00 P.M. SLEEP time.

2:30 P.M. TELEPHONE. Want to talk to GRANDMA?

3:00 P.M. Belinda's first step! Look who's walking! Look who's falling. Whoops! Sorry you're HURT/PAIN.

5:00 P.M. Time to make dinner. DON'T TOUCH the stove. It's HOT!

7:00 P.M. BOOK time. BATH time. TOOTHBRUSH time.

7:30 P.M. SLEEP time.

Do you get the idea? When you sign with your baby, just do what you would normally do and sign whenever it makes sense. Do what you can, as much as you can, and as often as you can, and you will get positive results.

But What If I Work Outside the Home?

Sure, that all sounds great for a stay-at-home parent, you say, but I have a full-time career!

The question is, it even possible to teach a baby to sign when so much time is spent away from him?

The answer: yes, it certainly *is* possible. Regardless of how many hours in the day you are away from your baby, you can still give him the gift of signing. You simply need to have a plan:

1. Make a list of all the caretakers in your baby's life. Do you have a nanny? Does a relative watch him? Do you take your child to a daycare center or preschool? Write their names down.

2. Start thinking about how you will educate and update everyone on that list. Make sure your strategy includes a regular method for them to update you on your child's signing progress and vice versa.

3. If your child is about to enter a daycare center or preschool, find one that is signer-friendly. There are many daycare centers and preschools that incorporate sign language into their curriculum. That's the ideal situation.

If not, why not get proactive? More and more daycare centers and childcare facilities are looking for ways to enrich their teachers' training and incorporate new practices to benefit their "students." Call on a few and get their reaction. There are many parents on the same quest as you are. Plus, childcare is a more productive and less stressful experience for teachers when they have a signing "clientele."

4. If you are using the express method to teach your baby to sign, getting your daycare or childcare center involved is more important than ever. As you know, the express method takes all the elements of teaching sign language and consolidates them into a two-week training session. It's important that everyone who comes into contact with your baby within that framework signs with him in a coordinated effort. Since many daycare centers use signing, this may not be a major problem for you. If you can't get the cooperation of your daycare center, just beef up your own efforts. Sure, it may take longer than two weeks, but it will happen. Just don't get discouraged.

Behind the Signs

Because parents are demanding it, an increasing number of daycare and childcare facilities are adding sign language to their curriculum. In addition to it being a great marketing tool, teachers are finding that their "students" are better behaved. See Appendix D for training opportunities for childcare providers.

5. If you can't find a situation that's signer-friendly, go to Plan B:

   ◆ Let your sitter/childcare teacher know from the very beginning that you are signing with your baby.

   ◆ Demonstrate the signs your baby is likely to use.

   ◆ Bring along a sign language book or something similar that you can leave each day for reference.

   ◆ Let your caregiver know which signs you're working on and ask her to be on the lookout for them. Ask for a daily verbal progress report.

♦ Keep the lines of communication open between you and your child's caregiver. Invite questions and promote a dialogue at every opportunity.

6. When you bring you baby home from daycare, sign as much as you can in whatever situations are natural and appropriate.

You *can* teach your baby to sign even if you're not with your baby 24/7. Will it take longer to see results? Perhaps. But with more people signing in more situations, it could even speed things up.

Initiate the Draft!

Regardless of whether you work in or outside the home, there's another valuable resource you should tap into to help achieve signing success. No matter what your situation, call for reinforcements!

SELECTIVE SERVICE NOTIFICATION

To: Grandma and Grandpa Jones
Grandma and Grandpa Smith
Big Sister Suzie
Big Brother Brucie
Brenda the Babysitter

You are hereby invited to convene at 2015 hours at the Mess Hall at 4124 Spruce Street to receive further instructions pursuant to your role in Operation: Baby Sign Language.

As loyal members of this company, we appreciate your ongoing commitment and dedication during previous missions and anticipate that same level of enthusiasm in assisting our smallest recruit.

John and Sally Jones, Co-Commanders

Headquarters Company

Why go it alone? Recruit the family for this major offensive. Not only will it make the process easier, it'll also make it much more fun. Remember the old adage about many *hands* making lighter work. It takes on a literal meaning in this case.

Because your baby will benefit from many role models, recruit as many as you possibly can:

◆ **Grandparents.** If you are lucky enough to have grandparents nearby, their involvement is critical. Chances are they never signed to you as a baby and may think the idea a bit off the wall. This means that before you teach them the signs your baby is making, you may need to convert them to the idea. Let them borrow this book or sit down with them apart from the rest of the family for a little one on one. Hopefully, your enthusiasm will be contagious.

◆ **Big brothers and sisters.** Be sure to include older siblings in the action. They'll love the attention they'll receive and will feel special teaching their little sibling something of real value.

◆ **Babysitters.** Because it's often difficult, if not impossible, to find a regular sitter, have new sitters arrive early on their first assignment so you can explain what you're doing and the importance of their role in it. The Baby Sign Language Journal that you'll find in Appendix E is a great resource for new sitters in interpreting what your baby may be trying to "say." Of course, don't just hand them the journal as you walk out the door. Demonstrate the signs yourself, leaving the journal for reference and reinforcement.

It's a good idea to educate everyone right from the beginning, if at all possible, before your baby is ready to start to sign. Encourage all recruits to read this book or at the very least have a general understanding of the process, make sure they know what your goals are, and keep them up-to-date on your baby's progress.

If you get new recruits after the mission has begun, bring them up to date right away. Make certain that they know the signs your baby is currently making—plus the ones that he hasn't caught onto yet. You never know who will be the first one to spot a new sign!

One final piece of advice about getting family members involved: I used the "initiating the draft" comparison because I thought it was a catchy way of getting the point across. But as you already know, no one is going to be motivated to join the effort if you act like a drill sergeant, making demands and not allowing questions.

The best "recruits" understand the mission and know how important their own role is in achieving it. So when you do have that family meeting, think of it as a fun family project, something you all can get involved in while doing something important for the littlest soldier. So, go easy. You can't afford for anyone to go AWOL.

Smart Signs

Place a copy of the Baby Sign Language Journal on the refrigerator or some other conspicuous place. By keeping it updated with your baby's progress, all family members and babysitters will know exactly what's going on.

Dealing With Naysayers

One thing that can really sabotage your efforts is people telling you that the whole idea of signing with a hearing baby is ridiculous. Others may say it's impossible, unnecessary, or even harmful. You know the type:

- ◆ "But, Joanne. I never signed with my baby. I just knew instinctively what little Bruno wanted. Maybe we were just closer to our babies in those days ...."

- ◆ "Look, it's only logical. You give your baby another way to communicate and you're going to be raising a mime. Might as well rename him Marcel Marceau."

- ◆ "Your baby has perfectly good hearing. Why treat him like he has some kind of disability?"

When you encounter people with attitudes such as these, you can either ignore them or try to convert them by sharing the research and the important benefits of signing. You might even loan them this book or give them a copy of their very own. How much energy you put into converting the ignorant or misinformed depends on how important they are to you and whether or not they have the potential to help you reach your signing goals.

Take Note

Don't let negative thinkers get in the way of progress. While it would be helpful to get support from the in-laws, for example, if you can't convince them, then move on without them.

You do need to realize, however, that some people are never going to open their minds to progress or change. You might talk 'til you're blue in the face and just won't win. If that happens, move on. You have other more important things to do—like signing with your baby. Don't waste your time listening to negative thinkers. They'll only sap your energy and enthusiasm. And who knows? Once they see how much fun everyone is having and see how responsive your baby is to the idea, maybe they'll see the light.

Do's, Don'ts, and Don't-Even-Think-About-It's

Now all that you need to do is—stay on track. You have all the tools and knowledge you need and your motivational level is high. But before I send you out there, let's review the key points you need to remember.

DO ...

- ◆ Speak as you sign.
- ◆ Sign only in context.
- ◆ Incorporate signs into your everyday routine.
- ◆ Repeat the signs you have taught.
- ◆ Get the family and other caregivers involved.
- ◆ Add new signs as your baby is ready.
- ◆ Use body language and real-life opportunities to reinforce what you've taught.
- ◆ Praise your baby for his efforts.
- ◆ Enjoy the experience!

DON'T ...

- Listen to skeptics and naysayers.
- Expect too much too soon.
- Show disappointment.

DON'T EVEN THINK ABOUT ...

- Quitting!

The Least You Need to Know

- The primary reason why babies stop signing is because their parents lost the motivation and quit.
- While signing may be repetitive at first, it's important to stay the course and keep your motivational level high.
- The best way to teach sign language to your baby is to incorporate signs into your daily routine.
- You can teach your baby to sign whether you are a stay-at-home parent or have a full-time career.
- For a more seamless signing experience, try to find a daycare center that already uses sign language in its everyday curriculum.
- Ask family members, babysitters, and friends to get involved.

Index

Signs Index

Dog	Hot
Don't touch	Hug
Down	Hurry
Drink	**I-J-K**
Dry	Ice cream
E-F	I love you
Eat	Jump
Elephant	Juice
Fall down	Kangaroo
Fish	**L**
Flower	Light
Frightened	Lion
Frog	Listen
G	Love
Gentle touch	**M-N**
Giraffe	Medicine
Good	Milk
Grandma	Mine
Grandpa	Mirror
Grass	Mommy
H	Monkey
Happy	Moon
Hat	More
Help	Music
Hide	No
Home	**O-P**
Horse	Orange

Wash hands

Water

Wet

Where

Wind

Work

Y-Z

Yes

Yours

You're welcome

Baby Sign Language
Dictionary

Beginning Signs

Beginning signs are listed here in their order of importance. They should be introduced to your baby in this sequence.

more

more

Bring the tips of your fingers together a few times.

eat

Your hand moves back and forth to your mouth as if eating.

eat

milk

milk

Your hand opens and closes as if you're milking a cow.

hurt/pain

hurt/pain

The tips of your index fingers touch.

help

help

Your open palms tap
your chest twice.
(Adapted from ASL
to make it easier for a
baby to model.)

help #2

help #2

One hand lifts the other
hand to represent the
concept of "assistance."
(Authentic ASL sign.)

diaper change

All fingers except your thumb fold to your palms. Bring your knuckles together and pivot in opposite directions. (This is the sign for CHANGE with "diaper" implied.)

diaper change

Food and Drink

Note: The signs for EAT, MILK, and MORE can be found in Beginning Signs. ALL DONE/FINISHED can be found under Potty Training.

apple

The knuckle of your index finger touches your cheek while your closed hand twists forward.

apple

banana

banana

banana

One hand "peels" a banana, represented by an upright index finger.

bottle

bottle

Pretend to grip a bottle with one hand and place it on the palm of your other hand.

breast feed

breast feed

Your flat palm lightly brushes the breast in a downward motion.

cookie

cookie

Your fingers make a circular motion as if using a cookie cutter on dough.

cracker

cracker

Tap your closed hand against your elbow.

drink

drink

Pretend you are hold-ing a glass and taking a sip.

ice cream

ice cream

Hold your hand as if you were holding and licking an ice cream cone.

juice

juice

Make the sign for "drink" and then fingerspell *J*, a downward hook made with your pinky.

orange

orange

One hand mimics squeezing an orange in front of the mouth.

water

water

Make a *W* with three fingers and place them at the corner of your mouth.

Good Manners

please

please

Your open hand makes a small circle over your chest.

sorry

sorry

Your closed hand makes a small circle over your chest.

thank you

thank you

Your fingertips touc
your mouth and the
move away from you
body.

you're welcome

you're welcor

Your flat open hand
moves outward from t
front of your face to y
waist.

Feelings and Emotions

Note: The sign for SORRY can be found under Good Manners.

angry

Your fingers bend while pulling away from your face.

cold

Your shoulders are hunched forward. Your hands shake as if they were cold.

cry

cry

The index fingers of both hands alternately trace tears rolling down your cheeks.

frightened

frightened

Your hand moves in front of your body as if you're trying to protect yourself.

happy

happy

Your hand moves upward on your chest, indicating "high spirits."

hot

hot

Your hand moves to your mouth as if you're about to eat. Then the hand turns and moves away quickly as if the food is too hot.

hug

hug

Both arms pull inward as if hugging something.

I love you

I love you

Extend your pinky, fore-finger, and thumb.

love

love

Use both hands to "hug" something over your heart.

sad

sad

The fingers of both hands are outspread and move down your face to your mouth.

Behavior and Safety

Note: The sign for HELP can be found in Beginning Signs. WHERE can be found under Independence.

bed

bed

Rest your tilted head on your hands.

clean

clean

One hand wipes "dirt" off the other one.

don't touch

A combination of NO and TOUCH. The index and middle finger snap to the thumb indicating NO. Then the middle finger of the same hand taps the back of the other hand (TOUCH).

don't touch

gentle touch

One hand gently "pets" the back of the other hand.

gentle touch

good

good

Your fingertips touch your lips and move slightly away from your mouth. (This can also be used for Good Job!)

listen

listen

Cup your hand to your ear.

no

no

The index and middle
fingers snap to the
thumb.

quiet

quiet

The index fingers start
at the mouth with one
hand in front of the
other. They then move
downward in a silencing
gesture.

share

share

One hand is held vertically with the thumb up. The other vertical hand slides back and forth over the index finger to convey slicing or dividing something.

sit

sit

The first two fingers of one hand "sit" on the same two fingers of the other hand.

sleep

Your hand is held in front of your face. Your fingers are then drawn to your mouth.

sleep

slow

slow

One hand moves slowly up the back of the other.

speak

speak

Your index fingers alternately move back and forth from your mouth.

stop

stop

Your flat hand is held vertically and drops forcefully on your other hand.

wait

wait

Your palms are held upward and your fingers wiggle. One hand is slightly in front of the other.

yes

yes

Your closed fist moves up and down.

Activities and Games

ball

ball

Your hands are open as if you're about to catch a ball.

book

book

Your palms open and close as if opening and closing a book.

computer

computer

Your hand is shaped
like a *C* and moves
along your forearm.

dance

dance

Your index and middle
fingers swing back and
forth over the palm of
the other hand.

fall

fall

Your fingers make a
V and stand on your
palm, then lie flat to
indicate falling.

hide

hide

With your shoulders
hunched, cup one hand
over the other with the
thumb peeking out.

jump

Your fingers form a downward *V* and jump up and down from your open palm.

jump

music

Your hand moves rhythmically back and forth over your arm.

music

paint

paint

The movement of the
fingers represents a
paintbrush applying
paint to a surface.

play

play

The thumbs and pinky
fingers of both hands are
extended and shake back
and forth.

run

run

Each hand forms a loose *L* shape. The index finger of one hand pulls on the thumb of the other. As both hands move forward the index finger wiggles.

swim

swim

Your hands and arms mimic the action of a swimmer.

swing

swing

Your index and middle fingers grab the same two fingers of the other hand and swing forward.

telephone

telephone

Your thumb is at the ear and your pinky is at your mouth.

walk

Three extended figures on each hand represent feet. The movement of the hands represents a person walking.

walk

Clothing

coat

Bring both arms forward as if putting on a coat.

coat

hat

hat

Your open hand pats
the top of your head.

pants

pants

The movement of the
hands indicates the
legs on a pair of pants.
Open palms slide down
both legs.

shirt

shirt

With your index finger and thumb, grab your shirt in the upper chest area and tug outward a few times.

shoes

shoes

Tap your two downward fists together twice.

socks

socks

Both index fingers point
down. One moves up and
the other down, brushing
against each other.

Family

mommy

mommy

The thumb of your
open hand taps your
chin twice.

daddy

daddy

The thumb of your open hand taps your forehead twice.

grandmother

grandmother

The thumb of your open hand taps your chin twice and then makes two arcs down and away.

grandfather

grandfather

The thumb of your open hand taps your forehead twice and then makes two arcs down and away.

sister

sister

One hand forms an *L* with the thumb touching the chin. It then moves downward to meet the other L-shaped hand.

brother

brother

One hand forms an *L* with the thumb touching the forehead. It then moves downward to meet the other L-shaped hand.

baby

baby

One arm cradles the other and both move side to side in a rocking motion.

Independence

Note: The sign for HELP can be found in Beginning Signs. STOP can be found under Behavior and Safety.

down

down

Your index finger points downward.

mine

mine

Bring your open hand to your chest to signify ownership.

up

up

Your index finger points upward.

want

want

Both hands are extended and then brought toward the body while the fingers curl up.

where

where

Wag your index finger
back and forth.

yours

yours

An open hand moves
toward the person you're
addressing.

Outdoors

clouds

clouds

Shape both hands like clouds.

dirty

dirty

The sign is similar to the sign "PIG" except fingers wiggle as if food is falling from one's mouth.

flower

flower

Draw your hand under your nose as if sniffing a flower.

grass

grass

Move your fingers toward your mouth with your thumb out to simulate an animal eating grass.

moon

moon

The hand is in the shape
of a C and taps the side
of the forehead.

rain

rain

Your fingers are spread
and fall downward at a
slight angle to look like
rain.

sun

sun

Shape your hand like a *C* and look up at it.

tree

tree

Your arm is upright and supported by the back of your other hand. Your upright hand pivots from the wrist to represent a tree.

wind

wind

Your hands indicate the movement of the wind by moving in a circular fashion.

Animals

alligator

alligator

Your hands open and close like the mouth of an alligator.

bear

bear

Your arms cross and make a clawing motion at your chest. (Use the same sign for Teddy Bear.)

bee

bee

Your index finger and thumb touch your upper lip and then brush across it as if brushing away a bee.

bird

bird

Your index finger and thumb open and close at the lips.

bug

bug

Touch your nose with the tip of your thumb. Your three middle fingers flutter to mimic the antennae of an insect.

butterfly

butterfly

Your thumbs lock and fingers flutter to look like a butterfly.

cat

cat

From the corner of the mouth, your index finger and thumb trace a cat's whiskers.

COW

cow

Your *Y*-shaped hand looks like a cow horn with the thumb touching your temple.

dog

dog

Snap your fingers together. Alternative: slap your thigh.

elephant

elephant

Your hand is shaped like the letter *C* at your nose and then slides down the body like an elephant's trunk.

fish

fish

The fingertips of one hand touch the wrist of the other and mimic the movement of a fish tail in water.

frog

frog

Your index and middle fingers flick outward under your chin.

giraffe

giraffe

Your hand makes a grabbing motion at your neck and moves upward.

horse

horse

Two fingers wave like the ear of a horse while your thumb touches your head.

kangaroo

kangaroo

Your hands are held outward and jump forward to mimic the hopping motion of a kangaroo.

lion

lion

With your hand shaped
like a claw, reach to the
opposite side of your
head. Then arc it back to
simulate a lion's mane.

monkey

monkey

Your hands scratch your
sides like a monkey.

pig

pig

Your hand flaps underneath your chin, representing food dropping from the mouth of a pig. (The sign is similar to DIRTY.)

rabbit

rabbit

With your hands facing backward, wiggle your index and middle fingers.

snake

Your index and middle fingers bend to simulate snake fangs and then move forward in several small arcs.

snake

spider

With your wrists crossed, link your pinky fingers and move your hands forward while wiggling your fingers.

spider

Bathtime

bath

bath

Your closed hand makes separate circular motions as if bathing.

brush hair

brush hair

Your hand simulates brushing your hair.

brush teeth

brush teeth

Your hand mimics the action of brushing your teeth.

bubbles

bubbles

Your palms are face down and your fingers flutter upward.

light

light

Your middle finger is
flicked in front of your
mouth.

mirror

mirror

Your hand is held as if it
were a mirror.

shampoo

shampoo

Mimic the action of washing your hair.

soap

soap

The fingers of one hand make a circle in the palm of the other to represent rubbing soap in the hand.

wash

Your closed downward hand circles your upward closed hand to simulate scrubbing.

wash

wash face

Make the sign for WASH, and then with your index finger, circle your face.

wash face

Potty Training

**all done/
finished**

all done/
finished

Both palms face toward
you and then turn over
and outward.

dry

dry

The forefinger wipes
across the chin as if dry-
ing it.

hurry

hurry

The index and middle fingers on both hands are extended and rapidly move up and down.

paper

paper

One hand brushes against the other hand.

potty/toilet

potty/toilet

Your index finger folds over your thumb. With the thumb peeking out, shake your fist back and forth.

wash hands

wash hands

The fingers of one hand make a circle in the palm of the other to represent rubbing soap in the hand.

Transportation

airplane

airplane

Extend your index finger, pinky, and thumb. Move your hand to simulate flight.

bicycle

bicycle

Your hands mimic the action of pedaling a bike.

boat

boat

Your hands form the
shape of a boat moving
through the water.

car

car

Hold your hands as if you
were gripping the steer-
ing wheel of a car.

train

train

The middle and index fingers of one hand cross the same fingers on the opposite hand and move up and down.

truck

truck

Hold both hands as if you were gripping a large steering wheel.

Places to Go

home

home

The *O* hand shape moves from the mouth to the cheek.

outside

outside

One hand comes out of a "hole" made by the other hand.

park

park

The index and middle fingers are spread and touch the upper side of the chest.

school

The hands clap twice to represent a teacher trying to get the attention of the class.

school

work

work

One closed fist taps the back of the other hand.

Miscellaneous

beautiful

Your open hand outlines the face as if expressing its beauty.

beautiful

big

big

Bring your hands apart as if describing something large.

broken

broken

Hold fists together and then sharply snap them downward.

medicine

The middle figure "mixes" medicine in the palm of the other hand.

present/gift

present/gift

The hands move forward in a gesture of giving.

small

small

Bring the palms together as if indicating something small.

teddy bear

teddy bear

Your arms cross your chest and make a clawing motion. (Same as the sign for BEAR.)

Part 3

The Advanced Signer

Welcome to the advanced class! Ah, but I see some *new* faces out there! You may be a little late to the party, but the important thing is that you're here now. Research has shown that children up to age three benefit from learning sign language. Plus, at your child's "advanced age," things will go much faster.

Without a doubt Part 3 is jam-packed with important information. Not only will you learn some valuable new signs that will help your baby (and you) make it through the "terrible-twos," but you'll learn invaluable techniques on how to incorporate sign language in potty training.

In this part we'll take a look at what happens when speech enters the picture. In some ways it's like the onset of the "talkies" when the silent film stars were quiet no more.

Chapter 8

Sign Language for Toddlers

In This Chapter

- Discovering why this is a good idea
- Learning a few tips before you get started
- Reading what other parents think about it
- Finding out how signing and talking relate
- Formulating your plan of action

A young family was recently tossed off a major airline because their toddler was throwing a major fit. The two-year-old ripped the in-flight magazines, kicked the flight attendant, and refused to sit down and buckle up. The parents complained to customer service that they weren't offered any time to comfort their child and rectify the situation. The airline apologized, booked them on the next flight, and upgraded them to first class. They also received a free round-trip ticket for future use. Apparently, the little tyke had something to say and didn't know how to say it. Perhaps if his parents had taught him a few basic signs, the story could have had a happier ending for everyone. Although the family would be minus the free ticket and would have had to ride in coach.

In this chapter you will learn that sign language benefits a toddler more than at any other age. Up to now, it has been a fun and rewarding experience—but when a child is between 18 and 24 months, sign language takes on a new dimension. He'll discover that while signs were useful to him before, now they're important. And if you think they're important to a toddler, you are about to discover that for you they're a godsend!

Studies have shown that children can benefit from sign language until the age of three—and maybe older. No matter where you and your baby are in his sign language education, you're in the right place. We'll help you continue your journey—or bring you up to speed.

Why It's a Good Idea

Let's get a bit more specific about why it's a good—no, make that *great*—idea to teach a toddler to sign. Most of you already know the answer, I bet. Or at least you have a pretty good idea.

Like most parents, you've heard about the benefits that signing offers and want in on the action. I suggest reading the beginning chapters if you haven't already done so. Here's the gist: when you sign with a baby or toddler, you stimulate more of his brain and open the door to a host of other developmental extras. Signing helps to accelerate language development, builds larger vocabularies, and makes learning to read easier.

On the emotional side, a signing child is less frustrated, has a closer bond with his parents, feels good about himself, and is having one heck of a good time. Signing is, after all, *fun!*

There are major plusses for parents of toddlers, too. One will become especially near and dear to your heart. Studies have shown that one reason for the so-called "terrible twos" is a child's inability to express himself. That can lead to trouble.

Behind the Signs

Studies show that everyone learns differently. Some are visual learners and others are more reliant on auditory information. When you teach a toddler to sign, he receives information both ways. This stimulates more of the brain and accelerates learning.

Information Overload

Learning to talk doesn't happen overnight. While toddlers are soaking up information and showing off what they've learned, their language ability is still quite limited and things get in the way of progress. This is the stage where toddlers are trying out new words, experiencing the power those words have, and beginning to realize that there is a whole new world out there on so many levels. One day they're experimenting with new words, the next day with exploring a new part of the house, and the day after, they're trying to figure how to climb up to the cookie jar or thinking about giving that new-fangled potty idea a try.

My point is that while toddlers are trying to become experts at everything, their focus won't always be on communication—until they need to get their point across. Yes, they may be communicating verbally to some degree—but the words they need may not always be there. Sometimes a toddler gets tired or maybe he says a word but no one can decipher it. Why, that can really upset a kid—big-time! What happens then? First he simmers, then he smolders, then he steams—and then he blows!! Look out, temper tantrum!

But if a toddler knows a few basic signs and he can use those signs to communicate what he wants or what he's feeling, well, you can see how that can help defuse things—and keep him from throwing an ear-jarring, teeth-shattering, blood-curdling fit on a airplane or in the middle of the cereal aisle.

Top Ten Reasons to Sign with a Toddler

Of course, there are other reasons to sign with a toddler. While I don't have any cymbals and drums at hand, I thought I would present them to you David Letterman style. It always helps to add a little sizzle to a presentation.

Ready? The Top Ten Reasons to Teach a Toddler Sign Language …
(Drum roll, maestro …)

10. It builds self-confidence and self-esteem.

9. Other toddlers use it and you don't want yours to be left out.

8. It gives additional emphasis to spoken words.

7. It helps overcome shyness.

6. It assists in expressing complicated feelings.

5. It beats crying.

4. It's better than temper tantrums.

3. It keeps bullies at bay.

2. It helps him get what he wants.

And the number-one reason to sign with your toddler …

1. It looks good on a preschool application!

Don't Take My Word for It

But let's stop talking in generalities. Here are some statements from
actual parents who understand what signing with a toddler is like, first
hand.

◆ "It's fun to do on a trip to the grocery store. Samantha can't wait
to get to the produce aisle so she can use the signs we taught her."
—Joanie K., New Orleans, LA

◆ "We taught our toddler a few animal signs before going to the
zoo. When we got there and saw a real elephant, Adam made
the elephant sign over and over. He was so excited!" —Amy Q.,
Bronx, NY

◆ "I observed Bobby in his preschool class. When someone took his
toy, he calmly went over, made the sign for MINE, and took it
away. I was thrilled!" —Peter G., Raleigh, NC

◆ "We saw many of the animals we knew the signs for at the circus. The next day, Annie made the sign for LION while eating breakfast. I guess she remembered it and wanted to talk about our trip. Amazing to think that before she could talk, she could initiate a conversation!" —Doris T., Clearwater, FL

◆ "Last night I made the sign for MILK without saying the word. I know, major infringement. But after I did, my daughter made the sign and then corrected me by saying, Milk, Milk." —Catherine P., Lewiston, NY

Smart Signs

Incorporate signs into your daily activities. Learn as many as you can ahead of time so you can be prepared when your toddler shows interest in something.

Your Job as Verbal Translator

As I've said, there will be times when your child won't be able to communicate verbally what he wants or needs. These are the times when signs are invaluable to him—and to you as important teaching opportunities.

Whenever your toddler makes a sign to get his point across, you should first show that you understand what he is trying to communicate. Then you need to take it to the next level and add verbal commentary. In effect, what you will do is to verbally describe what your child is unable to.

Here's an example. If little Sara is struggling with a wagon in the yard, she may make the sign for HELP. Your job, in that instance, is to say something like, "What's the matter, Sara? Are you trying to pull the wagon and it's stuck? You need HELP? I'll be glad to HELP! Let's pull that wagon together." Of course, while you're saying all that, you are demonstrating the sign. By doing this, you are indicating to your child that you understand her plight and showing her that you understand the sign she is making. More important, you are also serving as a model for future verbal language development.

Some Advice Before Getting Started

If you've been with me since the beginning of this book, you will have introduced the basic signs to your baby differently than we're about to demonstrate them here. No need to worry. Regardless of what you and your baby have done before, just follow the techniques or adapt them to what you are already doing. These alternative methods will reinforce what your baby already knows.

Here are a few tips to consider:

◆ Depending on your toddler's age, what you're about to learn may be more comprehensive than you need at first. Start slowly and move on to another lesson as you see fit.

◆ Select signing categories that make sense to you and will interest your child.

◆ Customize the material to the age of your toddler and your own daily routine.

◆ Teach signs in whatever sequence works best for you.

Smart Signs

Promote your toddler's verbal language development by adding verbal commentary to each signing situation. Your toddler needs to hear spoken language even more than he needs to see signs.

Your Plan of Action

I know you're anxious to begin, but first you need a plan. Think everything through before you make that jump and find you're in over your head:

1. If this is your first venture into the word of sign language, decide exactly *when* you want to begin introducing signs to your toddler. Once you begin, signing needs to be consistent.

2. Teach the Food and Drink category first, as it's the easiest and your child will catch on quickly. Good Manners would be the logical next step. You can take it from there.

3. Remember that it's not necessary to teach every sign in every category. Use whatever makes sense to you. Select the signs and categories that you want your child to learn and memorize them ahead of time. Taking it one category at a time will make it easier.

4. Rather than thinking of this as teaching *signs*, teach *associations*. Your child may be able to imitate your gestures, but he needs to know what they represent before he can use any of them meaningfully.

5. Meet with other family members for a practice session. Everyone must be familiar with the agreed-upon signs and ready to use them consistently.

6. Inform babysitters and teachers about the program and enlist their support. The more people who sign with your child, the better.

Take Note

Don't listen to anyone who says you can't go it alone! If you're a single parent or if other family members aren't interested, you can still teach your toddler to sign. While a group effort might make things go faster, the most important success factors are dedication, consistency, and love.

7. Concentrate on one category for at least a week before moving on to another. Then move on to other categories at your discretion. Trust your instincts.

8. As with anything else that you teach, repetition and reinforcement are key.

9. Keep things simple, natural, relaxed, and, by all means, enjoyable.

What About Talking?

In a book about teaching your baby sign language, it's easy to lose focus on teaching your baby to talk. Throughout the book I've tried to remind you that while teaching your baby sign language is an incredible thing, it's only a pit stop on your way to the finish line. Which gives me a chance to repeat the cardinal rule of baby/toddler signing:

always say the corresponding word as you sign—and encourage your toddler to do the same.

The toddler stage is a critical stage for verbal development. Around age one, babies start to talk—but their vocabularies have a long way to go. If they don't have the words at their disposal, signs can help tremendously. In addition, signing places an added emphasis on communication in general—not only for the toddler, but for the entire family. This helps explain why children who learn sign language speak earlier than their nonsigning counterparts. Their parents talk to them more. It's that simple.

The Least You Need to Know

◆ One of the primary advantages of teaching a toddler to sign is to reduce the frustration that comes with not having the right words at his disposal or not being understood.

◆ Children can benefit from learning sign language until they're about three years old and maybe older.

◆ Before you begin to sign with your toddler, make sure you are ready with a plan of action.

◆ Add verbal commentary to every signing scenario.

◆ As your toddler becomes more proficient in sign language, don't lose sight of his verbal language development.

Chapter 9

Learning by Example

In This Chapter

- Learning the most common teaching categories for toddlers
- Following step-by-step instructions for the most popular signs
- Finding out why teaching by example is the best strategy
- Discovering tips and techniques that can be applied to all signing categories

You and I have come a long way, baby! From the early days when we discussed the research and benefits of teaching sign language to your hearing baby, to the time when you actually taught your little one to sign. It's hard to believe that now he's a toddler and ready for more.

I think congratulations are in order for both of us: for you, because you've already achieved signing success and are still moving forward; for me, because I got you here! But maybe I'm being a bit premature with all the kudos. You still need to motivate your toddler to learn some additional signs—and I'm going to teach you how.

By the way, if you are joining us mid-book and haven't started any signing yet, it's not too late. I'm glad you've decided to join us. Your toddler is ready to communicate now!

Teaching Categories

There are many categories in this book that will prove to be of interest to you and your toddler. Here's the list of categories that you will find in the Baby Sign Language Dictionary:

- Beginning Signs
- Food and Drink
- Good Manners
- Feelings and Emotions
- Behavior and Safety
- Activities and Games
- Clothing
- Family
- Independence
- Outdoors
- Animals
- Bath Time
- Potty Training
- Transportation
- Places to Go
- Miscellaneous

Important Note: Because sign language can be so beneficial when it comes to potty training, I have devoted an entire chapter to it. Check out Chapter 10 for how to go about it.

For instructional purposes, in this chapter I have selected six of these categories to show you how it's done: Food and Drink, Good Manners, Behavior and Safety, Activities and Games, Feelings and Emotions, and Animals. The principles and techniques you'll learn can be easily adapted to any of the other categories. Refer to the Baby Sign Language Dictionary in this book to see how these signs are made.

Smart Signs

Illustrations and instructions for all signs are listed according to category at the middle of the book. For an animated demonstration of each sign and many more, visit the ASL browser at the University of Michigan's Communication Technology Lab. They have generously given us permission to cite their incredible resource. Go to http://commtechlab.msu. edu/sites/aslweb/browser.htm.

Food and Drink

When you teach the signs in this category, you'll be using a two-step approach. First you'll teach some generic signs that are associated with eating: EAT, DRINK, MORE, and ALL DONE/FINISHED. Once your toddler grasps those concepts, you'll present specific labels for the foods he wants (or doesn't want) to eat. See the Baby Sign Language Dictionary for the complete list of food and drink signs you can use.

Why is the Food and Drink category the best place to begin teaching your toddler to sign? It's because snacks and mealtimes are already part of your everyday routine. That makes them perfect "educational" opportunities. When you teach the signs in this category, you'll simply be capitalizing on an already positive experience, one that your child likes and looks forward to. When your toddler knows a few related signs, he'll have something else to make his snacks and mealtimes even more fun and interesting.

Take Note

Teaching in context takes on a whole new meaning in the Food and Drink department. When you teach a certain food sign, the object will obviously be there to help make the association. Just be sure to stock up ahead of time and be prepared when your toddler finally makes the sign himself. If you're out of apples when he makes that sign, handing him a banana will set your efforts *waaay* back.

Tips and Techniques

1. There is no right or wrong way to teach a sign. Your goal is to simply develop a natural way for your toddler to associate the sign with the idea that you're trying to convey.

2. You can teach the signs in the order that you'll find here or in any other way that seems logical to you. After all, it has to fit in with *your* routine. Make sure you learn all the signs in this category before you begin.

3. Introduce all first-step signs at one meal (EAT, DRINK, MORE, ALL DONE/FINISHED). Don't expect your child to remember them all right away, of course. While it may seem like a lot at first, think of it as a "signing showcase," a presentation of the signs that you want him to learn.

4. Make sure everyone is seated around a table where your child can see what's going on. Then demonstrate that it's time to EAT by showing the sign and taking a bite of something. Then ask another family member if he would like something to EAT. He responds that he would and says, "Yes, I would like something to EAT." He then demonstrates the sign and gets his "reward."

5. Then ask your child the same question. For example, "Bobby, would you like to EAT? I'm hungry. I think it's time to EAT." Every time you say the word, make the sign. Then reinforce it by either taking a bite of something or pretending to.

6. Introduce DRINK, saying and signing the word. Then take a drink of something. Have another family member do the same. Ask others if they would like a DRINK. They respond by signing and stressing the word. Repeat this a few times.

7. The next sign is MORE. Ask/sign if anyone would like MORE of something. When a family member responds that he would like MORE by using the sign, make sure he receives something.

8. To bring this lesson home to your child, give him one Cheerio and ask/sign if he would like MORE. Before he can get upset, give him another. Then repeat. This will help him to make the association. Make a game of this. Be happy. Smile!

9. Decide on which word(s) you will use (ALL DONE or FINISHED) and stick with it. When your toddler is finished, ask if he is ALL DONE. Do that a few times. Ask others if they are ALL DONE, and have them respond by making the sign before handing their empty plate to you.

10. Ignore the fact that this will seem awkward at first. What I have given you is the "shell" of the session. You need to add your own personality. By the way, you don't have to memorize your lines. (I hope you knew that!) Those were just ideas to get the idea across. In between each signing demonstration, act normal. Laugh and talk about other things. Once in a while when the time is right, add a signing demonstration. This has got to be fun for everyone.

11. Once you start using the signs in Food and Drink, continue to do so. With enough repetition, your family will feel more comfortable with the idea and your toddler will catch on quickly.

12. When you feel your toddler has a good grasp of those generic concepts, it's time to graduate to the next step and teach signs for specific food and drink items. But remember not to abandon the signs you have already taught. Continue to use them whenever appropriate.

13. Teach specific food and drink signs the same way as you did the generic signs. Show a BANANA, for example—make the sign and say the word. A day later, try the sign for JUICE. Repeat them often enough and your child will catch on. One day when you least expect it, he'll look at you and make the sign on his own. Make sure you have lots of everything handy. You don't want him to think that he's signing for no reason.

14. Introduce the other signs whenever you like. The important thing to remember is that you need to continue using the signs if you want your child to learn them.

Smart Signs

By 18 months your toddler should be speaking, or at the very least attempting to say words. Because your goal is to get him to sign and speak, never sign without saying the word. And don't anticipate your toddler's every need. Encourage him to sign *and* ask for what he wants.

Good Manners

PLEASE   THANK YOU

SORRY   YOU'RE WELCOME

The Good Manners category is the next logical step after Food and Drink signs. Regardless of whether they're spoken or signed, these concepts are difficult for a child to understand. We say PLEASE as part of a request for something, and THANK YOU when we get what we asked for. Then the person who gave us whatever we requested responds by saying YOU'RE WELCOME. Will this personally benefit your toddler? Maybe not at the moment. Just think of it as an early introduction to the rules of proper etiquette.

Tips and Techniques

1. Again, this has to be fun. A toddler's primary motivation for learning these words and signs is to "please" you! As there are no concrete associations for your child to make, he'll learn through habit. But he won't be motivated at all unless you make it enjoyable.

2. The best way to teach PLEASE and THANK YOU is to not make a big deal out of it. You are going to teach these signs by example.

3. While your child is at the dinner table with you, ask another family member for something—but use *lots* more spoken emphasis than you would normally. Then exaggerate the sign itself. For example, "Suzie, may I PLEASE have a napkin?"

4. When you receive what you asked for, exaggerate THANK YOU as you sign and smile.

5. Suzie's job isn't over. She now has to dramatically say and sign YOU'RE WELCOME.

6. Continue this strategy for a few days before you encourage your child to try it himself. Encourage him by gently taking his hand and guiding it through the signing motion. Only do this occasionally as a way to motivate him—but *never* force him to sign.

7. Results will depend on the age of your toddler and how often and consistently you sign with him. He may pick up the idea immediately, or it could take a few weeks. Stick with it, though, and remember to exaggerate your efforts.

8. Incorporate the signs into other parts of your daily routine. Whenever you say PLEASE or THANK YOU, make the sign. Add YOU'RE WELCOME whenever appropriate. Remember that your child needs to see other signing situations and applications to fully grasp how Good Manners signs should be used and in what circumstances.

9. SORRY is another sign that can be used throughout the day. Introduce it when there's a logical opportunity to do so.

10. Reinforce the SORRY sign with a long face and down-turned mouth to communicate your sorrow. As always, exaggerate.

11. Use SORRY when managing your child's behavior. Instruct him to tell others that he's SORRY about certain actions or behaviors and encourage him to use the sign.

12. Don't force the issue. Encourage your child to use signs, but don't demand it. For example: "Joey, wouldn't you like to say you're SORRY to Sarah? Maybe you'd like to show Sarah the sign, too?"

13. When your child responds by making the SORRY (or any) sign, give him lots of praise. As I said earlier, pleasing you is the primary motivation for making these signs in the first place. For example, "Joey, you made the sign perfectly! Keep up the good work!"

Behind the Signs

In one of my early workshops, a mother wanted her daughter to learn the signs in the Good Manners category before any others. There was just no way that she was going to raise an impolite child, she told me. I suggested that there were other signs that she (and you) should introduce first, because they have more immediate benefit—HURT and HELP, for example. Good Manners is icing on the cake.

Behavior and Safety

CLEAN	SIT
DON'T TOUCH	SLEEP
GENTLE TOUCH	SLOW
GOOD	SPEAK
LISTEN	STOP
NO	WAIT
QUIET	WHERE
SHARE	YES

The Behavior and Safety category has as many positive benefits for your child as it does for you. It enables him to exercise a sense of control over his relationships with others, promotes a better sense of self, and helps him grow as an individual.

Instead of pushing, pulling, and crying, a child can simply say or sign SHARE. Rather than letting himself be bullied, a child can just sign STOP. While this may not totally solve the problem (especially if the "bully" doesn't understand sign language), your little signer will feel more empowered and his overall body language will help convey his meaning.

Parents can use these signs as a way to reinforce positive behavior and to provide safety instructions. A physical gesture adds more clout to what you're saying, plus it motivates your child to pay closer attention to you.

Tips and Techniques

1. Because your child needs to make a personal connection (or association) in order for the light bulb to turn on over his head, wait for a situation when something negative occurs. (My bet is that you

won't have to wait too long.) Then deal one on one with the situation, using your tone of voice, facial expression, and body language to help convey your message—along with the sign.

2. The manner in which you model each sign will help get your meaning across. For example, STOP (the side of one hand coming down in a chopping motion on the palm of the other hand) should be made clearly, decisively, and emphatically, and then repeated, if necessary. It's the same thing with NO (your middle and index fingers snap to the thumb).

3. Remember to offer verbal praise to your toddler and to reinforce your approval with a sign: GOOD job! (Fingertips touch your lips and move slightly away from your mouth.)

Take Note

This is from the be-careful-what-you-wish-for department: don't be surprised when your toddler looks at you one day and gives you a double-whammy! Not only will he *tell* you that the answer is NO, but he'll also reinforce the fact that he means business by making the sign for NO at the same time. What are you going to do, wash his mouth out with soap, and his hands, too?

4. While this deviates from my normal advice, on occasion, silence can be golden. Take the following scenario: Let's say you're outdoors and you see your little Christopher on the other side of the playground. You see that he is pushing his way toward the front of the line to go down the slide. You can walk over there yourself, pull him out of the line, and admonish him in front of all the other children on the playground. Or you can simply call, "Christopher!" and with a disapproving look on your face, sign STOP or NO.

5. Introduce the other signs when it seems logical. Because signs need to be taught in context, wait for a relevant situation. In other words, wait for a situation when you would naturally say the word and then add its sign.

6. While the rationale behind most other signs is obvious, I need to make a few comments about a few of them:

◆ GENTLE TOUCH. This is a good sign to teach when a friend brings her infant to visit. Just as you use a stern voice for STOP, now your tone becomes calm and soothing. It's also a good sign to use when there is a new pet in the family. Many children like to grab or squeeze pets and need to be encouraged to take a more gentle approach.

◆ DON'T TOUCH. This is a combination of the NO and TOUCH signs. I'll bet it will become one of your most popular signs.

Activities and Games

BALL	PAINT
BOOK	PLAY
COMPUTER	RUN/CHASE ME
DANCE	SWING
FALL DOWN	SWIM
HIDE	TELEPHONE
JUMP	WALK
MUSIC	

By the time your child is a toddler, you really don't have to worry about bombarding him with too much information—or too many signs. Children's brains have an amazing ability to take in an incredible amount of information and sort it all out. It's like teaching words. You say a certain word over and over, emphasizing it as much as possible. When a child is ready and able to repeat it back to you, he will.

Tips and Techniques

1. The signs in this category will serve as an additional method and motivation for your child to express himself while adding to his signing vocabulary. Because many of these signs look like what they represent (iconic), they will be easy for your child and you to remember.

2. A brief demonstration is all you need to introduce the more obvious signs. The first time you read a book, show the sign for BOOK. "See how I can make my hands open like a BOOK? That's the way we make the sign!"

3. The same goes for BALL. "I'm going to make a sign and I bet you can guess what I'm signing. Yes, it's a BALL! Can you try?"

4. Promote the use of signs by asking your child to choose. "Do you want to play BALL or read a BOOK? Can you speak and sign your choice?"

5. Introduce MUSIC and DANCE together for their obvious correlation.

6. Sign PLAY and RUN/CHASE ME as part of your routine. Maintain a signing dialogue. "Would you like to PLAY? Let's see how fast you can RUN/CHASE ME."

7. Use books to teach the signs. Point to a picture, say the word, and demonstrate the sign. Ask your child to do the same.

8. Again, when it's appropriate for you to use a word and you know the sign, go for it.

Feelings and Emotions

ANGRY	HOT
COLD	HUG
CRY	I LOVE YOU
FRIGHTENED	LOVE
GOOD	HURT/PAIN
HAPPY	SAD

The benefits of encouraging your toddler to express his emotions by using words and related signs are obvious. When you do so, it validates his right to feel the way he is feeling. Plus, it gives him a way to let people know exactly how he feels, especially if he isn't able to articulate it. Simply put, signing reduces the alternatives: whining, crying, and kicking, to name just a few.

Tips and Techniques

1. As you're already doing, no doubt, continue to let your toddler know that having a certain feeling or reaction is fine—but that expressing that emotion by talking about it, and signing it, is even better.

2. Use books where characters convey specific emotions. Ask questions that promote a discussion of emotions and their related signs. "How do you think the three bears felt when they saw that Goldilocks ate their porridge? Do you think they were ANGRY? Have you ever been ANGRY?"

3. Consider creative role-playing to promote the use and understanding of different emotions and signs. Use body language and exaggerated facial expressions to better communicate the meaning of the signs. Play it up. Have fun!

4. While it isn't a true feeling or emotion, I have included the sign for HURT/PAIN in this category, as it's something that can result in crying or emotional upheaval. HURT/PAIN is a very important sign for you to know and teach. Because it's a bit more complex than some of the other signs, newcomers to the program should read more about how to introduce and reinforce the sign in Chapter 4.

Animals

ALLIGATOR	FROG
BEE	GIRAFFE
BEAR	HORSE
BIRD	KANGAROO
BUG	LION
BUTTERFLY	MONKEY
CAT	PIG

COW	RABBIT
DOG	SNAKE
ELEPHANT	SPIDER
FISH	

Sometimes in our endeavor to promote the use of signing to toddlers, we lose sight of the fact that it can be just plain fun! No, it isn't necessary that your child know the animal signs, but he will enjoy learning them—and you will, too.

Tips and Techniques

1. Introduce the signs for the various animals in a lesson devoted to the topic.

2. Model the sign for each animal using an animal picture book.

3. Reinforce the sign and the name of the animal by asking your child to sign and make the noise the animal makes.

4. Have your toddler make the sign and have others guess what the animal is.

5. Take your child to the zoo so he can show off what he has learned and see the "genuine articles" firsthand.

6. It doesn't matter what or how many animal signs you teach. Teach them just for the joy of it.

 Smart Signs

One of the best ways to reinforce signs is to make them interactive experiences for your child. When teaching your child animal signs, for example, a trip to the zoo takes on a whole new dimension. Not only will he see his picture-book animals come alive, but he'll have something to talk about for days. If he knows the signs, that is.

The Least You Need to Know

- There are no right or wrong ways to introduce signs to your toddler. If it feels natural, then you are on the right track.

- When you learn a sign language principle or technique, it can generally be applied to all signing categories.

- The best way to teach any sign in any category is to make it personal and relevant.

- Select signs and categories that are of interest to you and your child.

- Don't worry about bombarding your toddler with too many signs. With repetition and reinforcement, he'll sort it all out.

Chapter

10

Potty Training and Sign Language

In This Chapter

- Discovering why potty training and sign language go hand in hand
- Learning why you can potty train earlier with sign language
- Realizing why earlier is better
- Following some simple steps that make everything easier and less complicated

I guess we owe it all to Sigmund Freud. He's the guy who took a natural human function and created a universal obsession about it. Thanks to Freud, some people see the bathroom as a snake pit of psychological danger. If you scare or pressure your child when toilet training, he could end up with a phobia to last a lifetime. It could even affect his career choice, said Freud. If your training methods were too rigid, your child might become an obsessive-compulsive accountant. If you were too lax, he would be sloppy—and may become a painter! (He didn't specify portrait or house.) And that was only the beginning of the psychological mayhem that could result if you didn't get this stage of child training exactly right. Of course there was little or no scientific evidence to back up his opinions—but it sure scared the heck out of parents. And still does to this day.

Let me say right from the beginning that I'm not an expert on how to potty train children (although neither of my daughters is an accountant or a painter). My expertise is in helping parents and children communicate through sign language. But because one of the key elements of potty-training readiness and success is a child's ability to communicate his need to use the toilet, bringing the two together is as natural as the process itself.

How Sign Language Helps with Potty Training

In researching the material for this chapter, I came across numerous programs, theories, and philosophies as to the best way to potty train a child. (Do a Google search on "potty training" and see for yourself!) You'll find everything from elimination communication (EC) where a baby never uses diapers at all, to Dr. Phil's idea where you throw a potty party to train a toddler in a day. (Attention, event planners: a whole new market has opened up!)

Because it's not my mission to comment on the pros and cons of the different techniques or endorse one idea over another, I will instead refer you to the many resources available on the topic, some of which I have listed in Appendix D.

Behind the Signs

According to statistics, the average mom changes about 5,000 diapers in a child's lifetime. No statistics could be found regarding a dad's contribution. No, that's not an editorial comment. I simply couldn't find any numbers.

So now that I've told you what I *won't* do, what is it that I *will* bring to the table? It can be summed up the in one sentence, and it's an important bit of information: *regardless of how you decide to train your baby to use the toilet, sign language will make it easier, faster, and less stressful on everyone involved.*

Here's how:

♦ It makes your toddler feel as if he has more control in the process. The toddler stage of development is a time when children begin to realize they don't always have to do what you say. Using signs together helps promote a partnership rather than an adversarial relationship.

♦ It helps reinforce the potty-training routine. You know how toddlers love having you read them that same book over and over? It helps them feel in control when they know what the outcomes are. They also like regularities in their daily routine, and it's comforting to be able to predict what comes next. Because sign language in potty training consists of the same signs repeatedly, it reinforces the specific potty-training behaviors you are trying to teach.

♦ It alleviates some of the monotony. I think we all agree that potty training is not something we look forward to. In fact, based on my own experience as a mom, it's something you want to get over with as fast as you can. But when you think about it, it's probably not that much fun for a child, either. So if you vary the experience by signing while reading a book or singing a signing song, it could make the experience more enjoyable—for everyone.

♦ It eliminates some of the guesswork. Maybe your child isn't speaking yet, but it sure will make life easier if he can alert you to the fact that he has to use the potty. If a child can sign, there might be fewer accidents. That alone is worth the effort.

Smart Signs

When potty training, you'll use the same signing method as with any other signs. Introduce a relevant sign in context, say the word, and then repeat, repeat, repeat.

An Earlier Start

I've just discussed some important reasons to use sign language in conjunction with potty training, but the most important of them all is that it lets *you start earlier*. According to *Baby Signs* creators and baby sign language pioneers Drs. Susan Goodwyn and Linda Acredolo, whom you met in Chapter 1, potty training has gotten older over the years. In their book *A Parent's Guide to Potty Training*, they say that the main culprit is the disposable diaper. With disposables being available as large as size 6T, parents can wait longer, and because they do a remarkable job of keeping the little ones dry and comfortable, most toddlers don't seem to mind one little bit. Many may even enjoy the one-on-one personal valet service.

The other reason for the trend toward later potty training is that many pediatricians apparently fear the wrath of Freud and say to wait until toddlers decide to start on their own. Many parents take that advice and simply wait it out. I think you can see the problem with that. By the time parents finally say "enough is enough," some toddlers, many too big for their britches, want things to stay the way they are. You know what happens then.

It's About Being Ready

So where do things stand today? While Acredolo and Goodwyn recommend potty training before age two, most experts say to wait until a child is developmentally ready—with one of the primary benchmarks being whether or not he can communicate his need to use the toilet. Even if a child isn't saying a single word, sign language makes that communication possible. Goodwyn and Acredolo suggest that it can easily happen before the age of two.

The Readiness Checklist

When I use the word "readiness," I'm talking about cognitive and physical readiness as far as the potty-training process itself. You already know your child is ready and able to use signs—even if you haven't taught him any yet. Now let's see if he's ready in other areas:

♦ He stays dry for longer periods of time—for at least 2 hours or more—which indicates increasing bladder capacity.

♦ He recognizes when he is in the process of urinating or voiding.

♦ He is able to easily pull his training pants up and down.

- He can follow simple instructions.

- He is able to sit and focus on an activity for several minutes without becoming distracted or irritable.

- He shows interest, desire, and/or curiosity about the potty.

Potty Talk

How'd your toddler do on the checklist? Lists are great because they help consolidate a lot of information and give you some good guidelines based on the average kid. But as we all know, your child is unique and his signs of readiness may not even be listed.

Here are some snippets from parents who let me in on some private details. They're probably the same ones who will bring out the kids' naked pictures to show potential girlfriends and suitors:

- "I knew Anthony was ready when he toddled into the dining room with my husband's boxers on over his diaper."

- "It was apparent that Amy was interested because she kept flushing the toilet."

- "Seth started holding his nose when I changed his soiled diaper. It really helped that the smell bothered him."

- "Jacob was fascinated watching my husband urinate."

- "All it took was one Cheerio in the toilet to aim at."

 Take Note

It can take up to 500 years for one disposable diaper to decompose in a landfill—if it ever does. Even biodegradable diapers are not a solution because most times they don't receive the oxygen necessary for them to biodegrade. More reasons to potty train earlier!

Let's Get This Potty Started!

Okay, so now you're convinced that the idea of signing in this situation is a good idea. By the way, this is not a difficult thing to do. You do not need a lot of additional instruction to figure out how to introduce signs in potty training. Do just as you have always done. Simply sign and say "POTTY. Time to go POTTY," and then add the additional signs at the appropriate stage of the process. Then continue to reinforce the potty and signing routine repeatedly so it becomes habit.

The potty-training signs reflect the sequence that you use:

POTTY

PAPER

ALL DONE

WASH HANDS

GOOD

You can use these ancillary or secondary signs to vary the routine or introduce other factors involved when necessary, and they should be used to create and reinforce an awareness of the entire process:

DRY

HURRY

DIAPER CHANGE

Tips and Techniques

As with teaching your child anything, there are three steps involved:

1. Present your learning objectives.

2. Reinforce those objectives.

3. Reward success.

While signs can help you reinforce each of the three steps, it is not an exact science with a guaranteed recipe for success. So rather than a step-by-step approach, I've developed some suggestions and guidelines for you to follow:

◆ Start introducing all signs now. Many of them are applicable in any number of situations in addition to the bathroom. For example, ALL DONE, WASH HANDS, and GOOD could work as well at mealtime as they do at bathroom time. So if you haven't already done so, start introducing the signs into your everyday routine.

♦ If you have taught the sign for DIAPER CHANGE in Chapter 4, continue to use it. It will help create an awareness of the process— and bring enhanced awareness of the diaper when it's wet, dry, on, and off. If you haven't tried it, it could help.

♦ Pick a starting date and stick to it. Once you start to introduce signs at bathroom time, it is essential that you reinforce those signs and not let up.

♦ Once the child is on the potty, establish a sequence and stick to that as well. It's critical that you maintain the same routine every single time. The child will come to expect to see the signs and hear the words that go with them. He will come to realize what behaviors are expected with each sign.

♦ Once your child knows the signing sequence, you can introduce some ancillary signs as needed; for example, HELP or BOOK. (Sitting on the potty with a book is often a good idea and helps prevent boredom.)

♦ Keep an eye on your child to establish his bathroom routines and use that second sight mothers seem to have in predicting when their child needs to use the potty. When you get him out of the crib after a nap, for example, say right away, "It's time to use the POTTY!" Then make the sign. By the way, don't *ask* if he has to use the potty, just establish the routine without making it optional.

♦ When your child has experienced any level of success, be sure to praise him by the look on your face, with words, and, of course, the sign for GOOD!

The Reward System

The last step in the earlier list warrants additional attention. It is imperative that you make sure your child receives recognition for a job well done. There are many ways to do this, and each depends on what your child responds to best.

Acredolo and Goodwyn have developed a complete starter kit based on *Baby Signs* that not only includes an instructional book for parents, which I mentioned previously, but also a book for kids, a DVD with songs the child can sing, and a train whistle that he can blow as he "boards" the potty-training express. There are also stickers to give once a child has done "his business."

Of course, it isn't necessary to have all the bells and train whistles to potty train your toddler, but you do need techniques to motivate your child and reward his accomplishments. For some children, just your voice along with the big smile on your face will be enough of a motivator for him to continue. But other children respond better with visual reinforcement. A simple chart on the wall with smiley stickers on successful days can go a long way in helping you reach your goal.

Smart Signs

You don't have to wait until you've checked off every item to start training. Just look for a general trend toward independence and an understanding of what it means to go to the bathroom like a grown-up.

The Least You Need to Know

◆ Sign language makes potty training easier, faster, and less stressful for everyone.

◆ The biggest benefit of sign language is that it enables you to start potty training your child earlier, but wait until he is developmentally ready.

◆ Sign language instills confidence and competence and reinforces sequential potty-training steps.

◆ Teach potty training signs as you would any other signs.

◆ Make sure to reward your child for a job well done.

Chapter 11

Look Who Can Talk!

Teaching your baby to sign was a memorable experience, wasn't it? But let's not dwell in the past tense. You can still continue the process and keep teaching new signs. But even if you don't, he'll still use the ones he knows for quite some time.

By the way, you should definitely give yourself one giant pat on the back. You have done a *masterful* job constructing the bridge from his pre-verbal days to his first words. But your baby has only taken a few tentative steps across the great divide. We need to get him all the way there.

Keep on Signing

When your baby starts to say a few words, don't stop signing to him. In fact, encouraging him to sign will help him make the transition to spoken language easier.

According to *Baby Signs* researchers Linda Acredolo and Susan Goodwyn, babies can benefit from sign language until they're two-and-a-half years old. Other researchers say up to age three. They're still within that window of opportunity when their brains are primed for maximum stimulation in the language department. The longer you speak and sign with your baby, the brainier he'll become.

Think about that for a minute. If your baby said his first word at 12 months, for example, his brain will be positively impacted by sign language for another 18 months. And his brain will be *permanently* impacted by it throughout his entire life!

Why is that so? We've talked about it before, but let's go over it again. It's important. Spoken information (your voice) is received and stored on the brain's left side. Visual information (signs) is stockpiled on the right side. Because sign language involves both audio and video, so to speak, more of the brain is stimulated. When your baby needs to search and recall information, he has two sources to tap into. The result? A smarter baby with a larger vocabulary who'll also have an easier time learning to read. And that doesn't even begin to address the *emotional* benefits!

My advice? Just keep signing, baby. Continue to reinforce the signs that your baby already knows, and introduce new words and signs when opportunities present themselves. In other words, just keep doing what you've been doing. You're doing just fine.

Why He'd Rather Speak Than Sign

What will happen if you *stop* signing with your baby once he starts to speak? He will eventually drop his signs in favor of spoken words. Yes, he will have enjoyed the experience and benefited in so many ways— but his ultimate goal is speech. It's instinctive in all of us, after all. It's what we're programmed to do.

Like everything else, it will happen in stages. When your baby reaches a certain level in his development, the old way just won't be good enough anymore. Especially not when there's a *better* way.

The day will come, if it hasn't already, when your baby will want a more sophisticated way to communicate. Yes, sign language will have helped him, but soon he'll need more than just a way to label

Smart Signs

Why would a baby use sign language when he can speak? One reason might be for emphasis, to make sure that he's really getting his point across. He might use DON'T TOUCH, for example, when you want to change his diaper. Or NO when you tell him it's time to go to bed. Yikes!

things. While it still has a purpose—and may for some time to come—sign language will begin to lose some of its luster.

An Interview with a Signing Baby

Sometimes you get lucky. Just when I was racking my brain trying to think how I could best explain to you why a baby would choose speaking over signing, an expert dropped by who was willing to talk about it firsthand. I taped it for WCIG Radio so I could play it back for you. (That stands for *Complete Idiot's Guide*, in case you didn't figure it out.)

By the way, I agreed not to use his full name, as his parents weren't aware of his "speech tendencies" and he wanted to open that closet door at a later date.

> D.R.: Hello and welcome to WCIG Radio. Our guest today is Bradley the Baby. A big welcome to you, little guy! Can you tell us a little bit about yourself?
>
> Bradley: Well, there's not much to say. My life is only beginning, you know. I'm just 13 months old.
>
> D.R.: But I understand that within that short time you've become quite the little sign language expert.
>
> Bradley: You might say that. At first I was a little skeptical. I didn't really get what the hand signals were all about. But once I caught on, it made my life easier. Helped me get my point across. Less frustrated, you know. As you can see, I'm pretty relaxed.

D.R.: Why is it then that you're thinking of *quitting?*

Bradley: Take yesterday at the park, for example. There I was in the sandbox with two kids I'd never met before. They were a little older and actually saying a few words. One little girl gave me a pail and shovel and I signed THANK YOU. They both looked at me like I was from Mars.

D.R.: So what did that tell you?

Bradley: That not *everyone* knows sign language! Those two kids were into something I didn't know much about. So I asked myself, "How are you gonna communicate with people who don't know what your signs mean?" So spoken language is something I'm looking into.

D.R.: Well, it sounds like you already have an incredible grasp of verbal language.

Bradley: This is really all make-believe, you know. I'm not actually talking. We're only doing this to make a point.

D.R.: And the point is that because there are people who don't understand sign language, you'd better find a new way to communicate?

Bradley: Among other reasons.

D.R.: Such as …?

Bradley: It only works face to face. Yesterday I ran down the hall and signed MOMMY. I needed a DIAPER CHANGE. She was in the kitchen and couldn't see me. What good was sign language to me then? So I let out a howl and she came running. Sound is where my future is.

D.R.: Why, thank you, Bradley. You've been most informative.

Bradley: One more thing. I'm a busy kid. There's a lot of other stuff to do with my hands. Eating, of course, but then there's finger paints, toys, and, rumor has it, a new trike in my future. I just can't drop everything to sign. I think it's time to move on.

D.R.: So you're abandoning your signs in favor of speech?

Bradley: Well, *abandon* might be too strong a word, but I'm definitely gonna scale back once I make a little more progress using words. When I get real good at it, hasta la vista, baby.

D.R.: Out of the mouths of babes. Our guest today has been Bradley. Signing today—speaking tomorrow. And now a word from our sponsor ....

Whew! That little Bradley is really something, isn't he? Precocious little guy, but he makes a lot of sense and speaks for many kids his age when he tells us why he'll stop signing:

1. Not everyone understands sign language.

2. Sign language only works face to face.

3. Babies have more interesting things to do with their hands.

How It Will All Play Out

Your baby's signs won't disappear overnight. Most babies use them well after they've begun to talk and will keep them as long as they're useful. That's important to remember. As long as a sign helps a baby or holds some interest for him, he'll continue to use it. But it also means that while you may continue to reinforce his old signs or try to teach him new ones, if the signs aren't relevant or meaningful to *him*, you're wasting your time.

Why would a sign be useful to a baby when he's learning to talk? Well, maybe the word that he wants to articulate is multisyllabic. Try saying that sentence when you're 13 months old! Or perhaps he's just tired and he doesn't want to bother. Think of the reasons *you* use sign language. You don't sign? Maybe you don't use American Sign Language (ASL), but you *do* sign:

◆ You use signs for emphasis. "STOP right there and take off those muddy boots before you come in the house." It's much more effective when you hold your palm out in front of you, isn't it?

◆ What about when words just won't cut it? "I swear to you, the fish I caught was this BIG."

◆ When you take a giant bite out of a bagel with cream cheese and in comes Bobby. "Hey, Ma! Where's my ball cap?" If you know where it is, you point to it. If you don't, you shrug your shoulders.

◆ When you spot a friend across a crowded room and want her to TELEPHONE you later. Thumb to your ear; pinky to your mouth. (That *is* an ASL sign, by the way.)

Behind the Signs

Based on our instinctive ability to understand facial expressions, body language, and generic signs, a Japanese company has received a technology patent that would enable your car to convey feelings and emotions to drivers around you. That means that instead of honking and flashing your lights, your car would get its (and your) point across by crying, smiling, or grimacing. It would also eliminate the need for the universal sign of disapproval that many drivers use to critique the driving skills of others.

Your baby will continue to use signs for those very same reasons. For emphasis, clarification, and maybe, for a while, out of habit. When will he stop? It's hard to say. The crystal ball didn't work when you asked me when your baby would *start* to sign and it won't work now, either. As before, there are too many variables.

Regardless of when the transition to speech does occur, it almost always happens in stages. Of course, there are exceptions. There always are when it comes to a baby's behavior. But, generally speaking, here's what you can expect:

◆ Your baby will sign on his own without prompting.

◆ He'll say (or attempt to say) the word along with the sign.

◆ He'll drop most signs and keep a few favorites for clarification or emphasis.

◆ Words will take over and he'll drop the signs altogether.

You should be aware that at some point during the transition, your baby may have *two separate vocabularies*, one comprised of signs and another of words. He may devote all his energy to building his speaking vocabulary and not be interested in learning any new signs. He may be perfectly happy with the ones that he already knows. If you'd like him to learn a few more, try again in a few weeks.

On the other hand, he may be the type who just can't get enough. He wants to have it all. If that's the case, he may be open to learning new words *and* new signs. You just can't predict. Follow the leader.

Taking Corrective Action

Making the move from signing to speech is a complicated process for your baby. In effect, what he's doing is trading in one set of symbols (signs) for another one (words). Give him room to experiment with what works and what doesn't. But be vigilant! The signs he's making may be clues to what he's trying to say. They may help you to decipher his meaning.

At first, you should expect that your baby's signs will be more accurate than his words. After all, he has been signing much longer than he has been talking. Again, pay close attention to his sign and body language. When you can figure out what your baby is saying, it's less frustrating for everyone involved.

Here's another important tip: do you recall when your baby was beginning to sign and wasn't able to make the signs accurately at first? But you applauded his attempts anyway, right? Then you reinforced each effort by saying the word and showing him the correct way to make the sign.

Do the same thing now. If your baby says "Bah" for bottle, for example, show him how pleased you are that he is trying to speak. Maybe he has also made the sign for BOTTLE along with "Bah" so you know for sure what he's trying to tell you.

Let him know that you understand by making the sign for BOTTLE yourself. Then say something like, "BOTTLE! Yes, of course you can have your BOTTLE." Make sure you carefully say the word the way it's supposed to be said. Don't mimic his attempt. He needs to hear it the correct way so he has something to shoot for.

You and Your Baby's Secret Signs

There's another reason why you and your baby may want to hold onto some signs, even well beyond the stage when he has the ability to speak clearly for himself. Some signs may be—or can become—personal ways to communicate with one another without letting the rest of the world in on it ... well, at least the ones who don't sign, anyway.

Remember in Chapter 6 when you learned the sign for DON'T TOUCH? I mentioned that it could be a sign you and your baby could use when he got a bit older. When you were in a public setting and you didn't want him to touch something fragile, you could show him the sign. Better than a public tongue-lashing, don't you think?

Another suggestion is the sign for TOILET. When your take your toddler to the park, he may lose track of time and not think about going to the restroom until it is too late. Instead of embarrassing him in front of his little pals, occasionally flash the sign with an inquisitive look, to ask him to think about using the facilities.

Take Note

While silence may be golden in the "secret signs" arena, it's the only time you should offer a sign without its verbal equivalent. Signing without speaking will result in your child becoming a sign language expert. But will that help him recite the Gettysburg address or deliver a soliloquy on a Broadway stage?

Those are just two situations when it may pay to be silent. You'll discover some of your own. Maybe to remind him to say THANK YOU to Aunt Lucy for the sailor suit, as ridiculous as it might be. Or to ask him if he needs HELP with the bullies on the playground.

I received the following letter from one mom who talked about another special way to use a "secret sign." I found it to be especially touching and thought that you might enjoy it, too.

Dear Diane:

My daughter Kara and I had a wonderful experience learning to sign, and our entire family got involved. As she got older and her spoken language improved, she started to drop the signs that she had learned. While it was kind of sad to see them go, we were happy to hear her say one new word after another.

But there was one sign that she didn't drop. It was a sign that our family used then and continues to use today. It's the sign for I LOVE YOU. We got in the habit of using it whenever we would say good-bye.

This morning Kara got on the bus to go to kindergarten. It was not a day I was looking forward to, believe me. My baby was not a baby anymore! I went with her to the bus stop, trying to hide my tears as I watched her get on. As the bus pulled away from the curb, she bravely looked out the window at me, smiled, and made our secret sign.

Thank you for giving us all such a memorable experience.

Jane G.

Dallas, TX

Dealing with Speech and Language Development Concerns

Very early on in the book, I told you *emphatically* that when you signed with your baby, you had *absolutely nothing* to worry about as far as his language development was concerned. I also stressed that signing would promote your baby's language ability and that in no way would it hinder it.

So why deal with the subject if there is no correlation between signing and delayed language? Because many parents are concerned about it. It's a topic I'm often asked about. And because sometimes sign language can help children who actually do (for any number of reasons) have delayed language.

Just to make sure we're on the same page, let's start with some definitions. Exactly what is language and how is it defined? Simply put, *language* is the way we communicate with one another. It's a system of sounds and symbols that we use to express

Behind the Signs

While there may be any number of reasons why children have speech and language problems, none are caused by their having learned sign language as babies. In fact, a growing number of speech pathologists are using signs to augment traditional therapy and stimulate verbal language development in older children.

meanings, ideas, thoughts, and our inner feelings. In order to communicate with one another, everyone needs to know the symbols (words) and the rules on how these symbols go together (grammar).

Speech is part of language. It's a mechanical process that results in the formation of sounds and words. But speech is only one way that language is expressed. Writing and signing are others.

To help you understand the difference, let me hearken back to my days as a speech pathologist in the public school system. During that period, I had a large caseload of students, some of whom I was seeing for language disorders and others for speech disorders. Some language students had problems fully understanding what was said to them. Others had difficulty expressing themselves to others. Their speech was absolutely fine. It was processing the information that was giving them trouble.

The students who had *speech problems* had difficulty with the mechanics of producing particular sounds. Problems ranged in severity from a simple substitution problem ("wabbit" instead of "rabbit") to children who made so many substitutions and sound additions that their speech was almost impossible to understand.

The whole thing is pretty complicated. So what's a parent to do if you think there's a problem?

If you think your child isn't speaking when he should or not as much as he should, or if others have a hard time understanding him, consult the following timeline. Keep in mind that children speak and learn language at different rates, so the timetable is broad. That means if your child's behaviors don't match others of the same age, there may be no need to panic.

Speech and Language Development Timeline

Birth–3 months	Makes pleasure sounds (cooing).
	Cries differently for different needs.
3–6 months	Increased interest in sounds and voices.
	Responds to changes in your voice.
	Makes gurgling sounds.
	Babbling sounds more like speech and includes different sounds including *p*, *b*, and *m*.

6–9 months	Turns and looks in the direction of sounds.
	Understands that vocalizations get attention.
	Understands his first words.
	Can imitate gestures and manipulate objects.
9–12 months	Begins to understand simple instructions like "Wave bye-bye."
	Understands approximately 12 words by 12 months (names of family members, pets, body parts, basic clothing, etc.).
	May say his first word. Most babies speak their first words between 10 and 15 months. The average is 12 months.
	Recognizes words for common items like *cup*, *shoe*, and *juice*.
	Begins to respond to requests ("Come here," "Want more?").
	Uses speech and non-crying sounds to get and keep attention.
	Imitates different speech sounds.
	Has one or two spoken words ("bye-bye," "dada," "mama"), although they may not be clear.
12–24 months	Receptive vocabulary increases to as many as 300 words.
	Spoken language increases to an average of 200 to 275 words.
	Points to body parts when asked.
	Follows simple commands.
	Points to pictures in books.
	Says more words every month.
	Asks two-word questions ("go bye-bye?").
	Puts two words together ("more juice").
24–36 months	Vocabulary continues to grow.
	Ask "why" questions.
	Uses "no" and "not."
	Enjoys naming objects in picture books.

Source: The U.S. Department of Education

The Late-Talker Quiz

Still not sure whether your baby is developmentally on track? Then take the following "Late-Talker Quiz" and see if there are any potential problem areas:

1. Does your 18-month-old say any words clearly?

2. Does your 20-month-old follow simple requests like "Come to Daddy?"

3. Does your 24-month-old put two words together like "More juice?"

4. Does your two-year-old ask questions and respond to simple questions with "yes" or "no?"

5. Does your three- or four-year-old use language freely, experiment with verbal sounds, and begin to use language to solve problems and learn concepts?

> **Behind the Signs**
>
> Albert Einstein didn't speak until he was three or four years old. (No one knows for sure. His mother didn't keep a baby book, apparently.) He didn't read until he was seven and also had trouble remembering his address. Pianist Arthur Rubinstein was also a late-talker.

6. Do most people outside your family understand what your three-year-old is saying?

Now ask yourself this final question: do your instincts tell you that something is wrong? If the answer to this last question is "yes" and you answered "no" to any of the questions before it, then it's time to take the next step.

What to Do and When to Do It

If you suspect that your child has a language delay, it is not caused by teaching him sign language. Often we don't know the reason why a child is a late-talker. Rather than worry about what caused it, take action and get professional help to correct it. Talk to a pediatrician. Chances are, the doctor will refer you to a speech and language pathologist (SLP) who will evaluate your child with special tests. A hearing test will also be included to rule out the possibility of related-hearing problems.

Based on the test results, the SLP may suggest activities to do at home to stimulate development in this area. Often, that's all it takes. You may be advised to read more, use simpler words, and speak in shorter sentences to make imitation easier. You may also be encouraged to repeat what your child says, using correct grammar and pronunciation. This would enable you to demonstrate more accurate speech and language behaviors without directly correcting him. There are many different ways to tackle the problem.

Sometimes the speech and language pathologist will look at the tests, the age of your child, and the extent of the delay, and recommend group or individual therapy. If your child is having difficulty being understood, the pathologist might also recommend sign language to reduce the frustration that can result.

It's important to remember that some children are just slow speakers and simply need a bit more prompting. Sign language may help as an interim way for them to express themselves while stimulating their verbal language. If used properly, these late-talkers may speak sooner than they otherwise might have.

 Take Note

> It is *critical* that a speech and language pathologist make the determination about teaching sign language to children with delayed speech. Don't assume that sign language will help your late-talking child and take it upon yourself to start. Without professional guidance, your child may learn that there is little or no need to speak when sign language works just fine, complicating the situation even further.

Sign Language and Children with Special Needs

As you know, the focus of this book is to help pre-verbal *hearing* babies communicate with their parents through sign language. While sign language is a wonderful gift to give a child, a hearing baby will eventually learn to communicate without it. In other words, parents of hearing babies use sign language to enhance communication, not establish it. If you are the parent of a deaf baby, a more comprehensive and serious method of addressing the special needs of your child is in order.

In addition to the deaf and hearing-impaired, there are other special-needs children who may benefit from using sign language. Teachers and parents of children with Down Syndrome in particular have credited sign language with making a huge difference in children's communication skills as well as reducing their frustration.

Like all other kids, children with Down Syndrome develop at different rates, but, in general, all learn and develop more slowly than the norm. Low muscle tone and difficulty with tongue mobility affect speech production and can make speech difficult to understand. Add to that the fact that these children have trouble recalling and organizing information, and you can understand the major communication problems that can result.

Recent studies in this area appear to offer a new direction. Basically they say that while Down Syndrome children have difficulty learning with their *ears*, they can do much better learning with their eyes. In other words, instead of teaching them auditorily, teachers are using more of a visual approach.

Using sign language with children with Down Syndrome capitalizes on their visual strengths rather than trying to improve upon their weaknesses, so these children gain confidence and are less frustrated. Does verbal language take a back seat to sign language? Not at all. It's just another way of getting there. When children with Down Syndrome are taught visually, then auditory weaknesses also strengthen and speech gradually improves.

Behind the Signs

Down Syndrome is a genetic condition caused by extra genetic material from the twenty-first chromosome. It gets its name from the British doctor John Langdon Down, who first clinically identified the condition in 1866. The actual chromosomal nature of Down Syndrome did not become documented until 1959 by Dr. Jerome Lejeune. However, Down's name remains associated with the condition.

While Down Syndrome has received the most "press" regarding its success with sign language, there are other disorders that may benefit from it as well:

- Children with *autism* may also find it useful as a way to communicate.

- Due to the inability to control muscles, some kids with *cerebral palsy* find that sign language facilitates communication.

- Children with Attention Deficit Hyperactivity Disorder (*ADHD*) also benefit from the use of sign language. When they use their hands to communicate, it occupies their minds and gives them the ability to stay on task. That, in turn, enables them to better control their outbursts and interruptions.

Is sign language the ultimate solution or a panacea for children with special needs? Of course not. But it can be an effective tool. Parents and therapists who use sign language with special-needs children say it sure beats pointing and grunting. Because sign language is something that most children can learn easily, it also promotes positive situations that stimulate greater learning and, often, improved speech and language skills. Plus, sign language has the ability to decrease problem behaviors that may result when a child has trouble expressing himself.

The Least You Need to Know

- When babies learn that verbal language is more effective than sign language, they start to drop signs in favor of spoken words.

- Some babies continue to use signs to emphasize and clarify what they mean.

- Because children's brains are primed for language growth in the first three years, many parents continue to reinforce previous signs and introduce new ones after the onset of speech.

- There are some special signs that may serve you and your child beyond his early years and become "secret" ways for you to communicate.

- Children with delayed language may benefit from sign language, but only under the guidance of a speech and language professional.

- Special-needs children, such as those with Down Syndrome, may benefit from sign language, as it has been shown to stimulate verbal language development and reduce frustration.

Dad's Corner

A Dad's Special Role

I have to be honest. While I've tried to be unbiased throughout this book, I must admit that I've been directing my words to moms. And to all the dads out there, I apologize in advance, but, as you know, you are the exception to the parenting paradigm. If my experience has taught me anything, it's that moms are usually the ones to investigate the concept of baby sign language in the first place. They're also the ones to convince skeptical dads to give it a try. Of course, that's not always the case. At one of my workshops a few years ago, a young man walked in alone. He immediately caught my attention, as 99 percent of my attendees are moms and babies. Often a husband will accompany the family, but it's the women who make up the majority. Never before had a man come solo.

Sensing his awkwardness, I went over to him before the session got underway and introduced myself. Naturally I asked him how he became interested in baby sign language. He told me he was a single dad and that his wife had recently died. He said that they had discussed signing while she was pregnant and he wanted to teach his daughter how. Well, as you can imagine, I thought my heart would break. Yet it reinforced the fact that it is not only moms who play key roles in a child's upbringing—and motivated me to address the special role that dads play in their child's emotional and educational well-being.

And so, to the countless numbers of dads who are there from the delivery room to the dance recitals, to those who refuse to take a back seat in their child's upbringing, this one's for you.

Why Sign with Your Baby, Dad? Let's Count the Ways ...

In addition to all the benefits that signing itself presents, there are lots of reasons why dads in particular should participate in the process:

1. Your baby will learn faster if you and your partner are both involved.

2. It adds another level of interest and variety to the process.

3. Having another loving person responding to her signing efforts motivates your baby to continue.

4. Your participation gives your baby an opportunity to focus on you as a separate person with a distinct masculine presence.

5. It gives your baby early insight into your unique personality.

6. It establishes you as an active participant in your baby's life.

7. It adds greater value to the time you have together.

8. Signing creates a stronger bond between you and your baby—and between parents as well.

9. It enables you to play an engaging and more interactive role.

10. Signing establishes your role as educator and a great play date.

11. It gives you another reason to spend time alone with your baby.

12. It provides an element of structure to the time you spend together.

13. It starts an early communication bond and attachment.

14. It will delight your child—and you!

Tips to Help You Get Started

While you may not have as much time as you would like with your baby, maximize the time you do have:

- Learn how to sign together and coordinate your signing plan with your partner. If your partner is not interested, or is not present, go it alone.

- Keep updated on the signs that have been taught, along with your baby's progress.

- Be patient. This is not going to happen overnight.

- Create your own signing time with your baby and make it a routine. For example, read him a book and make animal signs. Or make bath time your time to play, bond, and sign.

- Rough it up. Add your own masculine personality to signing time. Roar and growl with the animal signs. Be loud and animated. Let your inner child out.

- Go on walks and outings together. Talk as you go, even if your baby doesn't understand. Pay attention to what he's interested in. Sign and talk whenever you can—and appreciate the time you have together.

One Special Dad

In Chapter 1 I talked about sign language pioneers and about how this whole baby sign language movement got started. If you haven't already read it, I think you may find it interesting—because the entire concept of signing with hearing babies got started because of one dad.

Joseph Garcia got the idea to sign with hearing babies based on his experience in the deaf community. Although he wasn't deaf himself, he had many friends who were and made an interesting observation. He noticed that the hearing children of deaf parents communicated much earlier than babies of hearing parents. Why? Because their parents had taught them a few simple signs. Using his two sons as "test subjects," Garcia began an incredible study to determine whether there were any benefits in teaching pre-verbal hearing babies to sign. His study prompted other serious studies and started an international baby-signing phenomenon. It prompted me to write this book—and you, to read it. Hopefully, it will motivate you to do even more.

Appendix B

Questions I'm Asked the Most

What's on Everyone's Mind?

Will sign language interfere with my baby's speech and language development?

On the contrary! Research has proven conclusively that babies who sign speak earlier and have larger vocabularies than babies who don't sign. Simply put, sign language will accelerate your baby's language development, not hinder it.

What will my baby be able to "tell" me?

Your baby can communicate when he's hungry, thirsty, or wants you to read another book to him. He can even let you know when he has an earache or needs a diaper change. It all depends on what signs you teach him.

When should I begin teaching sign language to my baby?

As a general rule, around six or seven months, but it's different for each baby. To determine if your baby is ready to begin, look for signs that your baby has enough long-term memory to remember the signs and the manual dexterity to imitate them.

How fast will my baby "catch on" to signing?

Again, each baby is different. In general, if you start when your baby is around six or seven months, you will see results eight to ten weeks later. It depends on your baby's age and how often and consistent your signing efforts are. The older your baby, the faster he will catch on. Babies who are 12 months or older may associate signs and their meanings in a matter of days.

When will my baby stop signing?

Most babies will stop signing when they find out that spoken words are more effective than gesturing. But some may keep a few signs to emphasize a point or to help them when they're not being understood. Again, it all depends on the baby.

What's the most important benefit of signing with my baby?

In my opinion, it's reduced frustration. When your baby is able to tell you what he wants or needs, he has little or no need to be frustrated. Life becomes less stressful for everyone.

How many signs will I have to learn?

That's up to you. We include over 120 signs in this program and have categorized them according to use. While there are some basic signs we recommend, after that it's up to you and your baby.

Do you use American Sign Language (ASL)?

Yes, our program is based on American Sign Language (ASL), the official language of the deaf community in the United States. It's a great way to start your baby on the road to being bilingual.

Can sign language of another country be substituted?

People from other countries have written to me to tell me they have successfully used British Sign Language (BSL) and Irish Sign Language (ISL) with the program. It doesn't matter which sign language you use. Just follow the guidelines in our program and substitute your sign language of choice.

My baby is in daycare. How will that affect his signing?

More and more daycare centers are using sign language to communicate with the babies in their care. Among other benefits, childcare professionals have discovered that there's less crying in a facility where babies sign. But even if your daycare provider doesn't offer signing expertise, you can still experience signing success at home. It may just take you a little longer. An even better idea? Try to convince your provider to get with the program!

My baby is over two years. Will he benefit from sign language?

A baby's brain is primed for maximum language development until the age of three. Plus, signing gives toddlers an outlet for expressing themselves when they can't come up with the words they need. So, the answer is a resounding "yes"!

Is it true that signing eliminates the "terrible twos"?

While signing may not *eliminate* the "terrible twos," it can make the stage more bearable! Because toddlers understand more than they can verbally express at this stage, they often become frustrated. The result is a wide range of negative behaviors, including temper tantrums. Sign language gives toddlers a viable outlet to express themselves.

We speak two languages in our home. Should we sign to our daughter in both languages?

What a wonderful opportunity for your baby! Make sure she hears and learns both languages. To make it easier in the early years, I suggest that one parent speaks and signs in English and the other communicates only with speech in the second language.

I have adopted a three-year-old little girl from Russia who speaks no English. Should I sign with her?

While signing won't hurt her and may even help reduce her frustration level, many parents in similar situations get too wrapped up in signing when the primary goal is to teach the child English. If you feel you can use signs as part of a support system, one that complements your verbal language efforts, then I suggest that you give it a try. But if you are nervous or unsure about it, then focus on verbal language alone.

I can't seem to understand what my baby girl is signing. What should I do?

It depends on the situation. Try looking for additional clues from her. What is she looking at when she's making a certain sign? What about her body language? That might also help you decipher what she wants. If you still can't figure it out, relax. It'll eventually click.

How do I motivate my baby to sign?

Try gently shaping his hands to make a certain sign or tapping them to give your baby the idea that you want him to use his hands to communicate. Just remember not to use or express disappointment when it doesn't happen. Your baby will sign when he's ready.

My baby is getting her signs mixed up. How do I correct her?

You correct her with repetition and by example. It's the same way you would correct her if she said a word incorrectly. If she is making the sign for SHOES when she means SOCKS, get out her shoes and sign and say "shoes." Do the same with socks. Do it a few times and she'll catch on!

My baby was making progress and now nothing is happening. What happened to his signs?

Maybe he has other things on his mind, like teething or learning to walk. Sometimes babies just take a signing "hiatus." The important thing to remember is for you to stay on track. Keep signing as before. Chances are, he'll be back.

How do I convince my spouse and other family members that this works?

Give them this book and highlight the research. But if that doesn't work, go it alone! It's too important an opportunity to pass up. My guess is that once the naysayers see how much fun you're having and how positively your baby is responding, they'll eventually join you in the effort.

What does it mean if my child uses signs without words?

It means that you're doing a great job! When that happens, show your pleasure by signing back to him, but say the corresponding word a few times to encourage him to do the same. In this instance, think of yourself as your child's verbal interpreter.

Doesn't adding sign language to potty training complicate the process?

Just the opposite. The signs will reinforce the routine and give nonverbal kids a way to communicate their need to use the potty.

Appendix C

Fun and Games

Activities to Encourage Your Baby to Sign

While signing should become part of your daily routine, activities and games that include the signs your baby already knows are an additional source of enjoyment for him. Plus, they'll serve as an effective reinforcement tool.

Baby Concentration

Cut out pictures of favorite and familiar objects. Make a copy of each one. Turn them over and play "concentration." This game is an ideal way to reinforce signs when you use pictures of signing objects (BALL, BOOK, etc.). Even if your baby can't discover the "pairs," do it for him, *talking* every step of the way as you select one object (sign) and then find its match.

Animal Cover-Up

Get out a favorite animal book and place a paper over a certain animal. Then sign the animal's name. For example, ask and sign, "WHERE is the LION?" Uncover the lion's picture and celebrate your "discovery," saying and signing, "There's the LION!"

Hide and Seek

Use the sign for WHERE with objects you hide. "WHERE is the BOOK?" or "WHERE is the SHOE?" Then watch your baby's amazement as you make the object magically appear! When he's old enough, let him look for and find the object himself.

Here's another variation: let your baby see you hide a BALL under a blanket and let him search for it (or you find it for him). Increase his attention span and signing vocabulary by hiding two or three objects at once.

Photo Album

Nothing works better than getting out the old photo album to teach signs for family members. Take your baby's finger gently and point to each member of the family while you make the sign and say the word. Make sure to point out his own picture to learn the sign BABY.

The Walking Tour

Take a walk around your house and "introduce" your baby to everyone and everything he meets. Stress the name of each object and, if you know it, add the sign.

The Good Night Tour

Make it a routine to sign and say goodnight to everyone and everything on the route to bed. After the family members, say good night to the dog, cat, even the telephone. Silly? You bet. But it's another opportunity to reinforce the signs you want your baby to learn.

Field Trips

A walk in the park, a trip to the zoo, an hour in the backyard. They're all educational signing adventures to your little one.

Grab Bag

Fill a laundry sack with signing objects like BOOK, BALL, TEDDY BEAR, etc. Then without looking, reach in the bag and pull out one of them. Make a show of it and act surprised when something comes out of the bag. Then sign and say the word.

Use Stand-Ins

While your baby is watching, "ask" his doll or Teddy if he'd like something to EAT or DRINK. Maybe he'd prefer MILK. Maybe poor Teddy bumped his head and is in PAIN. You get the idea.

Sing and Sign

Sing and sign to Itsy-Bitsy-Spider, Old MacDonald, and any other song you can think of. Or take a familiar melody and make up your own lyrics that include your targeted signs.

Read Books

Read as much as you can with your baby, adding signs as you go. Babies love repetition, so make sure you read the same book over and over.

Activities and Ideas to Stimulate Your Baby's Brain

Do whatever you can to provide new and varied opportunities and experiences for your baby. Every sight, touch, and smell stimulates his growing brain.

Play Imitation Games

When your baby is very little, imitate his babbling and facial expressions. As he gets older, play simple variations of "Simon Says."

Change His Outlook

Give your baby an occasional new outlook on life by varying the position of his crib or moving the position of his high chair.

Use Overhead Toys and Mobiles

Make sure there's always something available to intrigue and visually interest your baby.

Make a Foggy Face

Hold your baby up to a fogged mirror. As you wipe sections clean, talk about what you see as your baby's face magically appears.

Play Peek-a-Boo

This simple activity will stimulate your baby's brain, especially when you add some surprise variations.

Problem-Solve

Hide a favorite object under a blanket or pillow or in your pocket. Exaggerate your efforts until you find it. Let your baby or toddler participate in this problem-solving activity as he gets older.

Play Take-Away

Place three familiar objects on the floor and talk about each one. Then put a blanket over them while "secretly" removing one. Then remove the blanket and talk about the objects that are there. See if your baby looks for the one that's missing. As he gets older, increase the number of objects in the game.

Play Sequencing Games

Encourage your baby to imitate different clapping sequences and rhythms. Hold his hands and clap for him if he's not old enough. Or use colored blocks or colored cereal pieces as part of a sequencing activity. Say the colors out loud, "Blue, yellow, green. What comes next?" Then recreate the pattern. Make it a do-it-yourself game until your baby is old enough to participate himself.

Smell and Touch

Let your baby smell the differences between sweet and sour. Then let him feel something silky on his hand compared to something rough like sandpaper or a scrub brush.

Talk to Your Baby

Speak in sentences, have conversations, ask and answer your own questions if you have to—but make sure that your baby is bombarded with the sounds and rhythms of language.

Play Music

Play classical music around the house. It's a wonderful way to stimulate your baby's brain and class up your own act!

Play Comparisons

Line up things that are of the same category but different sizes. Three shoes, three plates, etc. Then put them in size order, saying "big, bigger, biggest." Mix them up and do it again.

Sign with Your Baby

I couldn't leave that out, now could I?

Appendix D

Resources

Online Resources

The Internet offers a wealth of information on sign language and early childhood education. The following have been selected as great places for additional research and valuable resources to make signing with your baby easier and more enjoyable.

American Sign Language (ASL) Dictionaries

ASL Pro (www.aslpro.com). An online American Sign Language dictionary that offers more than 6,000 useful signs.

ASL Sign Language Browser (http://commtechlab.msu.edu/ sites/aslweb/browser.htm). An extensive sign language dictionary of animated signs from the Communications Technology Lab at Michigan State University. A great complement to the Baby Sign Language Dictionary in this book.

Continued Instruction in American Sign Language

ASL University (www.lifeprint.com). A free resource for American Sign Language students, instructors, interpreters, and parents of deaf children. Hearing children may also benefit.

Signing Online (www.signingonline.com). Fee-based programs that provide the basics you need to become fluent in American Sign Language.

Speech and Language Disorders

The American Speech-Language-Hearing Association (ASHA) (www.asha.org). The professional association for speech-language pathologists and audiologists. Research information on speech and language disorders and delays.

Autism Research Institute (www.autism.com). Research and resources for parents of autistic children.

Down Syndrome Directory (www.downsyndrome.com). A directory of Down Syndrome organizations and comprehensive websites on the topic.

Speech Delay (www.speechdelay.com). A resource for parents and caregivers dealing with speech- and language-delayed children.

Early Childhood Education and Development

Healthy Start—U.S. Dept. of Education (www.ed.gov/parents/ earlychild/ready/healthystart/index.html). Twelve booklets, each focused on one month in a baby's life. An initiative of Laura Bush when she was First Lady of Texas; now revised and distributed by the U.S. Department of Agriculture, U.S. Department of Education, and U.S. Department of Health and Human Services.

Zero to Three/Brainwonders (www.zerotothree.org/brainwonders). A comprehensive and interactive resource for parents and early childhood education professionals on healthy development of children from birth to age three.

Baby Sign Language Forums

Parents and Educators at Berkeley (http://parents.berkeley.edu/ recommend/classes/sign_baby.html). Share your sign language experience with a California-based group of parents and professionals.

Sign with Your Baby **Online Forum (http://groups.yahoo.com/group/ signwithyourbaby).** Find parents and supporters of Joseph Garcia's *Sign with Your Baby* program.

Baby Sign Language Instructor Training

Baby Sign Language Instructors (www.kindersigns.com/bizopps. htm). An opportunity to learn more about joining the KinderSigns network of instructors and teach baby sign language in your own community.

Baby Sign Language Training for Childcare Professionals

www.kindersigns.com/www/Baby-Childcare-Edition.html. Information and instruction for childcare providers on how to enhance their curriculum with sign language for babies and toddlers.

Potty Training

Baby Signs Potty Training Starter Kit. Book, DVD, motivational materials. For potty training before the age of two. Search for keywords "Baby Signs Potty Training Starter Kit" for online resources.

Dr. Phil's Potty Party (www.drphil.com/articles/article/264). From Dr. Phil, the popular host of *The Dr. Phil Show.*

Elimination Communication (www.diaperfreebaby.org). A network of free support groups promoting a natural approach to responding to elimination needs by observing a baby's signs and signals.

Books for Your Baby

Bang, Molly. *Ten, Nine, Eight.* Greenwillow, 1996.

Brown, Marc. *Play Rhymes.* Puffin, 1993.

Brown, Margaret Wise. *Goodnight Moon.* Harper Festival, 1991.

Freeman, Don. *Corduroy.* Viking Juvenile, 1968.

Glazer, Tom. *Eye Winker, Tom Tinker Chin Chopper: 50 Musical Finger Plays.* Doubleday Books for Young Readers, 1978.

Hill, Eric. *Where's Spot?* Putnam Publishing Group, 2003.

Joosse, Barbara. *Mama, Do You Love Me?* Chronicle Books, 1998.

Keats, Ezra Jack. *Peter's Chair.* Puffin Books, 1998.

Layton, Meredith. *Baby's First Words* (Sign & Say Interactive Language Series). Peek-A-Boo Publishing, 1999.

Marzollo, Jean. *I Spy Little Animals.* Cartwheel, 1998.

Miller, Margaret. *Baby Faces.* Little Simon, 1998.

———. *Peekaboo Baby.* Little Simon, 2001.

Opie, Iona (editor). *My First Mother Goose.* Candlewick, 1996.

Oxenbury, Helen. *Clap Hands.* Little Simon, 1999.

Prelutsky, Jack. *Read Aloud Rhymes for the Very Young.* Knopf Books for Young Readers, 1986.

Tafuri, Nancy. *Have You Seen My Duckling?* Harper Trophy, 1991.

Touch and Feel: Home by Dorling Kindersley Publishing, DK Children, 1998.

Touch and Feel: Farm by Dorling Kindersley Publishing, DK Children, 1998.

Touch and Feel: Wild Animals by Dorling Kindersley Publishing, DK Children, 1998.

Williams, Vera. *"More, More, More" Said the Baby.* Greenwillow, 1997.

Books for You

Acredolo, Linda, and Susan Goodwyn. *Baby Signs: How to Talk with Your Baby Before Your Baby Can Talk.* Contemporary Books (a division of the McGraw-Hill Companies), 2002.

———. *Baby Minds: Brain Building Games Your Baby Will Love.* Bantam Books, 2000.

Daniels, Marilyn. *Dancing with Words: Signing for Hearing Children's Literacy.* Bergin & Garvey, 2001.

Garcia, Joseph. *Sign with Your Baby: How to Communicate with Infants Before They Can Speak.* Stratton-Kehl Publications, Inc., 2000.

Pantley, Elizabeth. *The No-Cry Potty Training Solution: Gentle Ways to Help Your Child Say Good-Bye to Diapers.* McGraw-Hill, 2006.

Appendix E

Baby Sign Language Journal

Keep track of your baby's signing progress by entering the date that you introduce a sign and the date when your baby masters it. Keep a copy on your refrigerator so babysitters or other caregivers can communicate with your baby when you're not at home.

More

Bring your fingertips together a few times.

Introduced: _____

Mastered: _____

Notes: _____

_____

_____

_____

_____

_____

Eat

Your hand moves back and forth to your mouth as if eating.

Introduced: _____

Mastered: _____

Notes: _____

_____

_____

_____

_____

_____

Milk

Your hand opens and closes as if you're milking a cow.

Introduced: _____

Mastered: _____

Notes: _____

_____

_____

_____

_____

_____

Hurt/Pain

The tips of your index fingers touch.

Introduced: _____

Mastered: _____

Notes: _____

_____

_____

_____

_____

_____

Help

Keep your palms flat and tap your chest twice. (Adapted from ASL.)

Introduced: _____

Mastered: _____

Notes: _____

_____

_____

_____

_____

_____

Diaper Change

All fingers except your thumb fold to your palms. Bring your knuckles together and pivot in opposite directions.

Introduced: _____

Mastered: _____

Notes: _____

_____

_____

_____

_____

_____

Bottle

Pretend to grip a bottle with one hand and place it on the palm of your other hand.

Introduced: _____

Mastered: _____

Notes: _____

_____

_____

_____

_____

_____

Drink

Pretend you are holding a glass and taking a sip.

Introduced: _____

Mastered: _____

Notes: _____

_____

_____

_____

_____

_____

All Done/Finished

Both palms face upward and then turn over and outward.

Introduced: _____

Mastered: _____

Notes: _____

_____

_____

_____

_____

_____

Water

Make a W with three fingers and place them at the corner of your mouth.

Introduced: _____

Mastered: _____

Notes: _____

_____

_____

_____

_____

_____

Down

Your index finger points downward.

Introduced: _____

Mastered: _____

Notes: _____

_____

_____

_____

_____

_____

Up

Your index finger points upward.

Introduced: _____

Mastered: _____

Notes: _____

_____

_____

_____

_____

_____

Use the following space to jot down notes to caregivers, progress made on specific signs, etc.

_____

_____

_____

_____

_____

_____

_____

_____

_____

_____

_____

_____

_____

_____

_____

_____

_____

_____

_____

_____

_____

_____

_____